THE BELLCREST SERIES

English for Business

TEACHER'S EDITION

London
OXFORD UNIVERSITY PRESS
1973

Oxford University Press, Ely House, London, W1

GLASGOW NEW YORK TORONTO MELBOURNE
WELLINGTON CAPE TOWN IBADAN NAIROBI
DAR ES SALAAM LUSAKA ADDIS ABABA
DELHI BOMBAY CALCUTTA MADRAS KARACHI
LAHORE DACCA KUALA LUMPUR SINGAPORE
HONG KONG TOKYO

ISBN 0 19 457110 6 (Student's Book)

English for Business was researched, developed and written by the Oxford University Press English Language Teaching Development Unit and produced in association with the BBC and the British Council.

Illustrations by Geoffrey Bargery

Printed in Great Britain
by Clarke, Doble & Brendon Limited

CONTENTS

TEACHER'S NOTES

The Series

English for Business is a corpus of teaching material related to the BBC and British Council series of films known as *The Bellcrest Story.* The course aims to train the skills of communication in English speaking, writing, listening and reading within a business context. It does not set out to be a handbook of commercial English, but concentrates on the practical application of English within common business and social contexts.

The course is a coherent series of lessons primarily designed for the teacher and a group of pupils to follow up and exploit *The Bellcrest Story.* It is therefore best used in conjunction with the film, although it can be used independently of it by the substitution of the taped version of the soundtrack of the film.

Level

The course is designed to cater for the requirements of people working in the more general areas of commerce, e.g. the Marketing, Economics, Personnel, Supply, Production and Administrative departments of industry. It does not cater for the specialist requirements of technicians or research staff, although they will find much that is of value in the course for their day to day work. It is assumed that pupils have already covered most of the fundamental grammar of English, either at school or at evening classes, but that there remain areas of weakness in the pupil's ability to handle English efficiently in the practical situations in which he finds himself during the course of his everyday work.

Size of Classes

The course is best suited to groups of between six and twelve pupils working under the guidance of a teacher.

The Teaching Situation

In order that the pupil may get the maximum benefit from the course, the following conditions within the teaching situation should be assured. Pupils should work in a group, and there should be between six and ten pupils in a group, preferably not more than twelve, for parts of the course (the role play).

It is assumed that pupils will be able to attend at least one, preferably two, double periods between each screening of the film. When the course is not used in conjunction with the film, it is assumed that pupils will be able to attend at least one double period per week. It is recognized that other time-tabling arrangements may be made to suit local requirements. Provision is made in the course for homework, and it is highly advisable that the pupils should be encouraged to do this.

The course is flexible to the extent that it can be used by groups attending either one or two sessions between each screening. Those parts of the course marked as being optional are designed primarily for those groups attending two sessions.

The course can also be used with groups of pupils of varying levels of attainment, in that provision is made for more advanced pupils in the course material, particularly in the language laboratory work.

The Form of the Course

On completion of the course the pupil will have increased his general business vocabulary considerably. His ability to listen to and understand native speakers conversing will have noticeably improved, as will his ability to handle English in the more common business situations. His ability to both read and write business English will also have improved.

The course consists of

1 The film of *The Bellcrest Story*, or a tape of the soundtrack of the film.

The film consists of thirteen episodes of approximately twelve minutes each, and is a business adventure story for television. Each episode tells a chapter in the story of Bellcrest Ltd., a fictitious company near Leicester, in England, that manufactures electronic components. The 'story' is that of the development and financing of a new product, the SC1, an AC speed control device for electric vehicles. The film has a 'hero', the Marketing Manager, who is responsible for the project. In the course of his fight for the SC1 he meets a great many difficulties, including bitter competition from a rival company, dissension inside Bellcrest itself, the uncertainty of a Merchant Bank's advancing the vital loan to finance the project and a fire that destroys a large part of the factory. The story moves to a climax in the thirteenth episode, when the Bank's decision is made and the fate of the SC1 is decided.

2 The Teaching Material

The main course consists of a Teacher's book, a Tape Companion containing scripts of the recorded drills and passages for Aural Comprehension, and a Pupil's Book. There is a set of thirteen tapes that accompanies the course, each tape accompanying one unit. The pages lettered a, b, c and a key to the Written Exercises appear only in the Teachers' Book.

The films do not contain any overt teaching sequences. The purpose of the film is to expose the pupil to areas of language in readily comprehensible and common business situations, such as meetings, visiting customers both at home and abroad, production, supply and delivery problems, and entertaining. The situations portrayed in the films, and the difficulties faced by the characters, are then exploited by the teacher in the classroom according to the needs of his group.

The main course consists of thirteen units. Each unit consists of

1 A summary of the episode last screened or listened to
2 Exercises
3 Structural Drills
4 Dialogue
5 Gambit Drills (optional)
6 Role Simulation (optional)
7 A passage for Aural Comprehension (optional)

The parts of the course marked 'optional' are intended for those groups who have two double periods between each screening of the film. They are 'optional' in the sense that a teacher will probably not be able to handle them as well as parts 1–4 in one double period alone. With certain classes the teacher may of course prefer to substitute one of the 'optional' sections for a section earlier in the unit.

3 The Grammatical Content

The grammatical work in the course should be regarded as remedial. The course does not set out to provide a complete 'grammar syllabus', but concentrates on those grammatical items that learners of English find difficult to master and most frequently misuse.

The items dealt with in the course are

Verb Tenses: Formation of the Present Simple
Present Simple contrasted with Present Continuous
Formation of the Past Simple
Past Simple contrasted with Past Continuous
Past Simple contrasted with Present Perfect
The Present Perfect
The use of the Future Tenses
Reported Speech
Indirect Questions
Formation of the Passive
Impersonals and Obliques
The Gerund as a Noun
Gerund v. Infinitive
Conditional Sentences
The Modal Verbs
Verbs followed by an Infinitive
Tenses and Time references

General: Comparison of Adjectives
Adjective v. Adverb
Position of Adverbs
Comparative with 'than'
Adjective plus Infinitive
'There is' v. 'It is'
'Used to'/'be used to'
'Much'/'many'/'a lot of'
Connectives

4 The Summary

The purpose of the summary is to re-present the language used in the film for the teacher to deal with thoroughly with his class. The teacher will find Comprehension Questions in the Unit Summary of each episode designed to elicit use of the key words and structures dealt with in the unit as a whole. The teacher will readily find further areas of useful language in each summary not immediately covered by the Comprehension Questions, and is encouraged to expand these to suit the needs of his group.

The summaries are purpose-written to the extent that they contain many examples of the structures and lexical items to be dealt with in the unit, and therefore provide a springboard for the teacher into the grammatical work of the unit. They are also complex in order to give the pupil practice in reading and understanding passages of English of a standard that he will probably meet in reports, articles etc.

5 The Exercises and Structural Drills

The exercises are of two kinds, lexical (Vocabulary) and grammatical. The lexical exercises are so designed that there is often more than one possible alternative, and they should therefore provoke discussion on the shades of meaning introduced into sentences by the use of various alternative words.

The grammatical exercises and structural drills should be viewed as complementary to each other. Both are designed to provide practice leading to mastery of the grammatical items they contain. It is hoped that the teacher will work out his own oral introduction to each structure dealt with in a unit to suit his individual group.

Where there could be any doubt as to how to use the exercises or structural drills, the teacher will find guidelines on individual exercises and drills in the 'Additional Notes' section of each Unit Summary.

6 The Dialogues

These are taped dialogues within specific business and social situations. There are three forms of dialogue used in this course:

Episodes 1–5

a The pupil listens to the complete dialogue
b Repetition of key words and phrases leading up to complete utterances
c Simultaneous repetition of one character's utterances
d Active participation

Episodes 6–9

a The pupil listens to the complete dialogue
b Repetition of key words and phrases leading up to complete utterances
c Active participation with books closed

Episodes 10–13

a The pupil listens to the complete dialogue
b Repetition of key words and phrases leading up to complete utterances
c Participation
d Multiple choice. Here the pupil has a choice of expressions printed in his book, and is invited to use alternative expressions in a second participation.
The purpose of the dialogues is to provide not only practice in pronunciation and intonation, but also an introduction to the use of the gestures and gambits of English within clearly defined situations. By 'gestures' and 'gambits' is meant such expressions as 'I wonder if I might raise a point here', 'Not at all', 'Wouldn't

it be better if . . .' that are so frequently used by English people to signal manoeuvres in discussions and negotiations and are therefore important for the learner, but that cannot be adequately treated as 'structural' items.

Provision is made in the course for the expressions in the dialogues to be actively used by the pupil in situations which demand their use – the Role Simulation. The Dialogues can therefore be viewed together with the Gambit Drills as a preliminary to the Role Simulation.

7 The Gambit Drills

These are more complex and demanding on the student than the structural drills, and it is suggested that the teacher should consider carefully whether all or only some of his class are able to handle them satisfactorily.

These drills are designed for the pupils to practice intensively the ways in which an Englishman expresses himself when he wants to signal a 'manoeuvre' or 'gambit' during the course of negotiations or a meeting, or a discussion. The drills are contextualized, in that they place the pupil within a specific situation, such as a meeting, where the use of the gambit being drilled is appropriate.

The teacher is strongly recommended to encourage his class to use these gambits in the Role Simulation, thereby giving pupils the opportunity of employing them in the natural context of free conversation and discussion.

8 Passages for Aural Comprehension

These passages are designed to improve the pupil's ability to listen to and understand native speakers conversing in a natural way. The teacher will find a passage for Aural Comprehension on each tape. This consists of a conversation or discussion on a business topic between two or more native speakers. The teacher will find a transcript of each passage in the Tape Companion, where he will also find the Comprehension Questions based on the passage reproduced.

9 The Role Simulation

Each unit contains a 'Role Simulation', consisting of a Statement of Problem, Description of Roles and a Written Follow-up. The material in this part of the course is designed to activate and improve the pupil's ability to handle English within common, clearly-defined business situations.

This is done by adopting the role simulation approach widely used on Management Training Courses, where a specific business problem is put before a group, to which a solution must be found based on lifelike discussions/negotiations leading to collective decisions. Each member of the group is allotted a specific role, e.g. Marketing Manager, in the light of which he must actively participate in the discussions/negotiations and contribute towards collective decisions.

The teacher is urged to do the Role Simulation, where time-tabling permits, as this part of the course provides a framework within which the pupil can generalize, and re-apply the structures, vocabulary and gambits practised in the unit as a whole. For this reason it is best handled as the last activity in each unit.

10 Homework

Each unit contains two items for homework, an exercise (Exercise E in each unit) and a written follow-up to the Role Simulation.

The Materials and Their Use

1 Diagram of Contents

Materials / Activity	Pupil's Book	Tape	Teacher's Book	Tape Companion
Presentation	Film/T.V series on sound-track tapes			
Review of the film Comprehension Oral Activation	Summary text		Summary text Comprehension questions	
Structural exercises and drills	Exercises Drill notes	Drills	Exercises and key Drill notes	Drillscript
Dialogue practice	Dialogue text	Recording of dialogue with exploitation		Complete script
Gambit drills	Drill Notes	Drills	Drill notes	Drillscript
Aural comprehension	Written questions	Recording (3–5 mins) of a discussion/interview etc.	Written questions	Complete script written questions and keys
Role Simulation	Statement of problem		Statement of problem Description of Roles	
Homework	Exercises E and written follow-ups to Role Simulation		Exercises E and written follow-ups to Role Simulation	

2 Presentation of Materials

The suggested order in which the material is best presented is:

a The Film, or the tape of the soundtrack

b The Summary with Comprehension Questions

c The Grammatical Content of the unit, both in the classroom and in the language laboratory.
d The Dialogues and Gambit Drills
e The Aural Comprehension
f The Role Simulation

It is left to the teacher to calculate the amount of time he will need to spend on each part of the unit according to the needs of his individual group. It is recognized that adjustments to the above order of presentation of the material may well be necessary to suit local conditions. Such adjustments are left to the discretion of the teacher.

3 The Summary

The summary is best handled immediately after the screening of the film. Pupils may, if desired, be requested to prepare the summary before the screening of the film. With a weak class this will aid comprehension of the film, though it will of course reduce the impact of the story line in the film.

4 The Exercises and Structural Drills

It is suggested that the lexical exercises are best dealt with orally immediately after handling the summary, as many of them deal with areas of related words which may pose difficulties for the pupils in distinction of meaning and usage. They can also be written for homework as reinforcement. There is also an 'exercise' for homework, usually in the form of a letter. Pupils should be strongly encouraged to do the homework, as practice will increase their ability to write English within a business context.

The exercises can then be done either orally in class as supporting material for the teacher's introduction, or as homework for revision purposes. It is recommended that structural drills should be seen as practice material for the establishment of the structure within the pupil's working knowledge of English, and they should therefore be used as a reinforcement of the teacher's work in the classroom. A possible approach to each grammatical item would be:

First Step: Oral introduction by the teacher, leading from selected sentences in the summary.
Second Step: The relevant exercise done orally in the class (or as homework).
Third Step: Intensive oral practice in the language laboratory (using the appropriate structural drill).
Fourth Step: Generalization, either worked out by the teacher or done through the medium of the Role Simulation.

It is recognized that this scheme may not fit all timetabling arrangements, and it is left to the teacher to adapt the practices outlined above to suit his own requirements.

5 The Dialogue and Gambit Drills

These are best handled after the structural drills. Pupils should be encouraged to use the expressions in the Role Simulation.

6 The Passages for Aural Comprehension

These passages are best dealt with in the language laboratory, where the pupil can stop his tape to answer the questions in his own time, although they can also be handled with a tape recorder in the classroom.

7 The Role Simulation

Where no specific recommendations are made in the Additional Notes to a unit, the Role Simulation is best handled as follows:

a Study of the Statement of Problem. It is vitally important that the pupils fully understand the problem they have to solve. If desired, pupils can be asked to look through the text before a lesson in order to save classroom time.

b On completion of the Statement of Problem, allot a role to each pupil in the group. When allotting roles, it is advisable to bear in mind the pupil's actual work and use of English in real life.

c Pupils should now be allowed time to prepare their roles. Where time-tabling permits, this should be done as homework; where not, the teacher should allow 15–25 minutes of classroom time for this purpose.
The teacher will notice that the Descriptions of Roles occur only in his book, and not in the pupil's book. This is because there is frequently information in individual roles of a confidential nature, and for all members of the group to have access to this detracts from the effectiveness, not to mention the enjoyment, of the confrontation.

d Faction Meetings

Pupils are usually required to prepare their roles individually. There are occasions in this course, however, when a 'Faction Meeting' is necessary. Where it is necessary, the teacher will find it stated in the Additional Notes. A 'Faction Meeting' is essential when the members of the Group divide into two or more teams representing two or more different companies, and therefore working together. The purpose of the Faction Meeting is to give the representatives of the two opposing sides in the confrontation a chance to meet apart from each other and to work out a common approach to the problem to be solved and to decide on the tactics they will adopt to get what they want out of the opposition. Preparation of individual roles is then done after the Faction Meeting and in the light of the decisions reached at it.
If possible the two or more factions should hold their meetings in different rooms.

e The Confrontation

The problem should now be fully discussed and acted out. The whole discussion should be recorded so that in the follow-up both pupils and teacher may refer back to selected segments of the discussion to illustrate and discuss salient language points.

f The Role of the Teacher

The role of the teacher changes from the moment the pupils embark on the 'Faction Meetings' (where held) or Confrontation. Experience has shown that it is highly inadvisable for the teacher to interrupt, whether to correct a mistake or for any other reason, during the course of a discussion as it detracts from its tempo and atmosphere. During discussions the teacher therefore acts as an observer.
Mistakes can be followed up by the teacher in two ways. He can either equip himself with a pad of paper and note mistakes as they crop up, or he

can record the discussions. Recording has shown itself to be the more effective way as far as the pupils are concerned. Although it is recognized that to listen to and select passages from such recordings takes up a lot of the teacher's time, experience has shown that to be able to recall selected mistakes and have them corrected in context is of great benefit to pupils.

g **Teacher's Follow-up**
Regardless of how the teacher records mistakes made during the course of discussions, the teacher should follow these up as soon after the discussion as possible. Action should be taken according to the nature of the mistakes made.

h **Pupil's Follow-up**
There is a task for homework directly related to the Role Simulation that the pupils should be strongly encouraged to do.

i **Additional Roles**
The number of roles given for each unit is ten. Where a teacher has less than ten pupils in his group, pupils may be asked to take two related roles, e.g. Managing Director and Assistant to the Managing Director. Where there are more than ten pupils in a group, the teacher should add the requisite number of roles himself. This can be done quite easily by, for example, dividing one role into two parts, by giving one or two of the leading characters an assistant or by inventing a completely new role.

THE STRUCTURE OF BELLCREST LIMITED

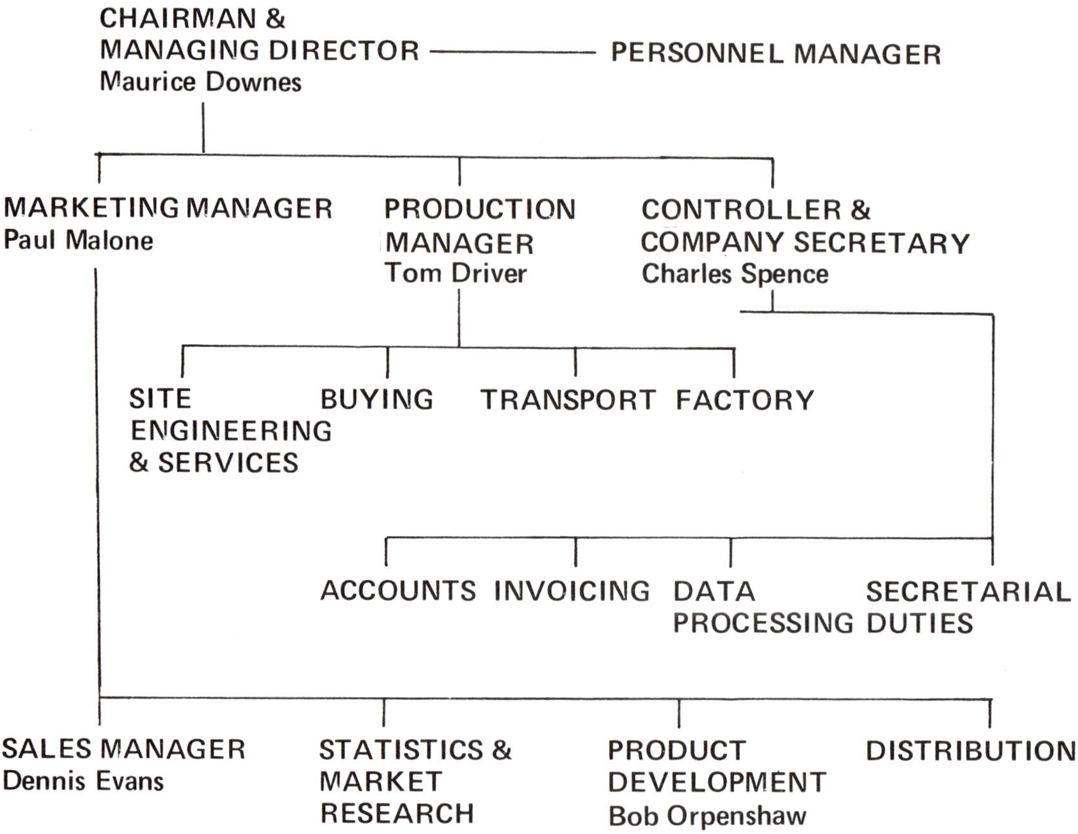

DIVERSIFICATION

George Hanson, a journalist writing a series of articles on successful companies, visited Bellcrest to make a case study of the firm. Bellcrest Limited is a medium sized company with its factory and offices near Leicester in the English Midlands. It manufactures electronic components for computers and communications and control systems.

Hanson learned that five years ago Bellcrest was in financial difficulties, because it had been concentrating on the research and development of new products rather than on marketing them. Ashburnham's, the merchant bank, made a loan of £300,000, at a low rate of interest, and bought a percentage of the shares. They put Edward Needham, Sir Frederick Ashburnham's assistant, on the Board of Directors and appointed Maurice Downes as Chairman and Managing Director.

As Downes and the Marketing Manager, Donald Williams, disagreed on policy over discontinuing certain products; Williams was forced to resign and Downes appointed Paul Malone in his place. Downes reduced the range of products and concentrated on making better use of resources and on more efficient production

As a result of his policy, annual sales have increased rapidly during the last five years, and the sales output per employee has almost doubled; Bellcrest is now a successful profit-making concern. Hanson also learned that Malone is looking out for opportunities to expand and diversify while Downes is very cautious about changing his policy.

At a meeting at the Bank, Sir Frederick Ashburnham expressed his satisfaction at Bellcrest's recovery, indicated by the rise in share prices and the increase in the final dividend. He told Downes that, in Edward Needham's view, Bellcrest no longer needed the loan, and the Bank might decide to withdraw it in order to reinvest the capital with an expanding competitor with development plans.

Downes was taken aback at this news and had to agree to let the Bank have detailed proposals of Bellcrest's development plans within the next two months in the hope of persuading the Bank to allow Bellcrest to keep the loan.

Downes' first course of action after this unexpected turn of events was to call at Malone's home the same evening. He instructed Malone to look at all Bellcrest's development projects and to report back to him with his recommendations.

UNIT SUMMARY

Structures

The structures dealt with in this unit are:

1 The Present Simple:

He works for Bellcrest.
He doesn't work for Bellcrest.
Does he work for Bellcrest?

2 The Past Simple:

He went to London.
He didn't go to London.
Did he go to London?

3 Comparison of Adjectives:

slow/slower
efficient/more efficient

Vocabulary

The areas of vocabulary dealt with in this unit are:

1 Investing 2 Competition 3 Market 4 Job Applications (an exercise supplementary to the Role Simulation).

Additional Notes

Exercise D

This is a two phase oral exercise. In the first phase the pupils are invited to make single sentences. *e.g.*

'Bellcrest's products are *reliable*'

In the second phase the pupil's statement is countered by an objection from a second pupil, e.g.

'Bellcrest's product's are reliable.' – first pupil.

'True. But on the other hand our company's products are *more* reliable.' – second pupil.

Drills

As many pupils may not have used a language laboratory before, it is advisable to practise the mechanics of at least drill one before taking the group to the laboratory. To do this the teacher can give the stimuli orally in the classroom and drill the pupils in the appropriate response pattern.

The function of the 'notes' for drills three and four should also be pointed out.

Role Simulation: 'An Interview for a Job'

The Role Simulation in this unit is different to that in all the other units. The purpose of the Role Simulation in this unit is twofold. It is primarily designed to introduce the pupils themselves to Role Simulation within a context with which all pupils should be familiar. It is advisable that the teacher should explain the approach to be adopted, and spend some time on this, as it is unlikely that pupils will have experienced this method before on language courses. In a method which demands initiative and imagination from the pupils themselves, it is necessary that each pupil have a clear idea of what is demanded of him. This unit therefore aims to introduce the pupil to Role Simulation within a known situation.

Secondly, by allowing the pupils complete freedom in their use of language, it enables the teacher to assess the existing language abilities of his pupils within a much shorter period of time than is normally possible.

Procedure

1 Introduce the Statement of Problem.

2 There is a supplementary exercise on the area of vocabulary required in the context of an interview for a job that may be used if desired.

3 Divide the class into two or three groups of three/four pupils each, depending on the size of the class. Each group will take it in turns to be the selection board, the candidates and observers. Each group should then be allotted an appointment to interview for when its turn comes to be the selection board, taken from those listed in the Statement of Problem. One of the remaining groups should be delegated as candidates, and the other as observers. A cycle is thus set up for which an appropriate description of roles should be distributed, e.g. for nine pupils.

Appointment	Group A	Group B	Group C
Transport Manager	Selection board	Candidates	Observers
Personnel Manager	Observers	Selection Board	Candidates
Dep. Co. Secretary	Candidates	Observers	Selection Board

Allow ten minutes before the first set of interviews for candidates and selection board to prepare. Suggested points to take up are given in the description of roles, although naturally pupils should be encouraged to expand on these. Further preparation can be done by groups when they are observers.
A selection board should interview one candidate at a time. It is advisable to set a time limit of ten minutes to each interview. To help pupils 'arrange' their interviews, there is a suitable form printed in the pupils' book.
Mistakes of language should be corrected by the teacher at the end of each interview.
The room should be arranged to simulate an office as far as possible.

COMPREHENSION QUESTIONS

1 Who is George Hanson? **2** Why did George Hanson visit Bellcrest?
3 What was Bellcrest's financial position five years ago? **4** Why?
5 Who rescued Bellcrest? **6** How?
7 What else did they do? **8** What is Downes' position?
9 What position did Williams have? **10** Why did he resign?
11 Who took his place? **12** What was Downes' policy?
13 What results did it have? **14** What does Hanson learn about Downes' policy for the future?
15 Is Malone of the same mind? **16** Who did Downes see at the Bank?
17 What evidence did the Bank have of Bellcrest's recovery? **18** Does the Bank intend to let Bellcrest keep the loan?
19 Why? **20** What was Downes' reaction to this news?
21 What did he promise the Bank, and by when? **22** Where did Downes go after his meeting at the Bank?
23 What did he tell Malone to do?

EXERCISES

Exercise A Complete the following sentences:

1 An ______ is a man who puts his money into a business. If he i. ______ his money in a company, he usually buys ______ in that company and is known as a ______. Instead of a fixed r. ______ of i. ______ he usually receives a d. ______ on his capital.

2 Unless a company holds a monopoly, it has to ______ with rival firms. The existence of ______ is a factor no company can ignore; indeed, many companies keep a constant eye on the activities of their ______

3 Before a company decides to introduce a new product it must ensure that there is a ______ for it. To find out whether it can ______ the product, a company will often conduct a m. ______ s. ______. Most companies have a M. ______ M. ______ who is in charge of sales promotion.

Exercise B Make sentences from these notes:

Examples:

Bellcrest/make/electronic components?

Does Bellcrest make electronic components?

Malone/want/diversify/product range.

Malone wants to diversify the product range.

1 Orpenshaw/work/research and development department.
2 Downes/carry/heavy responsibility.
3 Evans/not/Board of Directors.
4 Bellcrest/manufacture/electronic components?
5 Ashburnham/not/want/continue/loan/Bellcrest.
6 When/you/want/my report?
7 Downes/not/understand/Needham/arguments.
8 He/delay/every decision/until/too late.
9 You/have/plans/development?
10 We/not/know/why our products/not/sell.

Exercise C Complete these sentences:

1 Five years ago Smith & Co. only (manufacture) ______ bicycles.

2 They always (sell) ______ most of their products on the home market but (export) ______ some of them to Africa.

3 In 1968 foreign competition (increase) ______ and sales (drop) ______ sharply.

4 The Board of Directors (feel) ______ that the company (must) ______ diversify.

5 They (plan) ______ to get a loan from the Bank and as the company (enjoy) ______ a high reputation, they (have) ______ no difficulty in getting one.

6 They (spend) this money on development and (begin) production of motorcycles a few weeks ago.

7 Hanson (write) a very interesting article on Bellcrest.

8 Bellcrest (take over) a smaller company last year.

9 Their competitors (read) about it in the Financial Times.

10 One customer (buy up) our complete stock.

Exercise D Make sentences from the table below:

Example *a) Bellcrest's designs are reliable*
b) True. But on the other hand, Davidson's designs are more effective.

	designs		effective
Bellcrest's	marketing techniques		good
	products		successful
Our company's	production methods	is / are	efficient
	salesman		quick
Davidson's	service		slow
	delivery		bad

Exercise E Written Task

When Downes returns to Bellcrest after his meeting with Sir Frederick Ashburnham at the Bank, he has to write a letter confirming the points raised during the discussion. You write this letter for him. Use these notes:

Surprised at possible withdrawal of bank loan.
Agree to produce development plans within two months.
Trust no action will be taken until then.

DRILLS

Drill 1 The Bellcrest works are in London, I believe.
NO, ACTUALLY THEY AREN'T IN LONDON.

Oh, surely they make electrical machines.
NO, ACTUALLY THEY DON'T MAKE ELECTRICAL MACHINES.

Drill 2 I wonder what products Bellcrest manufactures.
YES, WHAT PRODUCTS DOES BELLCREST MANUFACTURE?

And I wonder why Williams resigned.
YES, WHY DID WILLIAMS RESIGN?

Dialogue *George Hanson arrives at Bellcrest.*

Hanson: Good morning, I have an appointment to see Mr. Malone, the Marketing Manager, at 11.15.

Hanson: Hanson. George Hanson.

Hanson: Thank you very much.

Hanson: Yes, that's right.

Hanson: How do you do? I hope I'm not putting you to any trouble.

Drill 3 Notes:

1 The works
2 Our sales company
3 Managing Director
4 Supplement
5 You
6 An explanation
7 Their contract
8 The Board

Drill 4 *Paul Malone is introducing his associates to visiting journalists.*

1 Managing Director/Downes
2 Sales Manager/Evans
3 Chairman/Downes
4 Company Secretary/Spence
5 Head of Research/Orpenshaw
6 Personnel Manager/Jenkins
7 Production Manager/Driver
8 Transport Manager/Mackenzie

ACTIVE LISTENING

George Hanson, a journalist, is questioning Malone about Bellcrest.

1 How much did Hanson know about the history of Bellcrest before he talked to Malone?

2 Why did Downes have to put the company back on its feet?

3 What was Bellcrest's reputation before Downes came?

4 Why didn't Bellcrest have enough money to continue their research five years before?

5 What action did the company then take?

6 Why was Edward Needham appointed to the Beilcrest Board?

7 How long did Downes wait before cutting out unprofitable lines?

8 What does Malone think about Bellcrest's present markets?

9 What details does Malone give Hanson about new fields he plans to go into?

10 What is Hanson's reaction to this?

ROLE SIMULATION

Statement of Problem

When Downes introduced his new policies designed to put Bellcrest back on its feet, it was not only Donald Williams who resigned. There were a number of resignations from men occupying key positions within the company.
The posts that fell vacant at that time were those of Personnel Manager, Transport Manager, Distributor Sales Manager, Supply Manager, Deputy Company Secretary and Deputy Head of Research and Development.

Bellcrest advertised these posts and received a great many applications. On the basis of the curriculum vitae submitted, a short list of three candidates was drawn up for each post, and those selected were asked to attend an interview. Downes formed a selection board to conduct the interviews consisting of himself, Paul Malone and Bob Orpenshaw.

The problem confronting the panel is therefore to select the most suitable applicant of the three applying for each post.

Written follow-up

You are Downes. Write two letters to two of the candidates you have interviewed, one offering the candidate the job, the other rejecting the candidate.

DESCRIPTION OF ROLES

Maurice Downes

You are the Chairman of the selection board and are therefore responsible for leading each interview. You may allot particular areas of each interview to Malone or Orpenshaw. Remember you will have to decide which candidate to appoint.

Malone

You are the Marketing Manager and should approach each interview with your marketing requirements firmly in mind. You are free to invent your requirements.

Orpenshaw

You are the Head of Research and Development and should approach each interview with the needs of your department firmly in mind. You are free to invent your requirements.

Each member of a selection board

Before you interview a candidate, you should work out your attitude to the following points:—
The salary you will offer.
The qualifications you require for the job.
What value to put on the candidate's previous experience.
The prospects you can offer at Bellcrest.
You should think up some other points to raise with the candidate.

Each Candidate

Before being interviewed you should think out an imaginary curriculum vitae.
You should also work out your attitude towards such questions as:—

Salary.	Holidays
Prospects with Bellcrest	Reponsibilities

You should think up other points which you may wish to raise at the interview.

Supplementary Exercise

Complete the following sentences:

1 When you see an advertisement for a job, and you want to a.   for the job, you send in an a.

2 You usually enclose a c.   v.   with your letter.

3 If there are a great many c.   for a single job, a company usually draws up a s.   l.

4 Candidates are then asked to come to an i.   , which may be before a s.   b.   or with a single person.

5 The a.   is made on the basis of the interview and r.   from people who know the candidate.

Name		Date of Interview:
		Time

Married/single age children

Health

Willingness to travel

Manner and Appearance

Education and Qualifications (summarize)

Present Position

Experience

Administrative ability

Social ability, relationships

Ability to work under stress

Initiative

Motivation (goals)

Leisure Activities and Interests

Present Salary

Date from which available

Expenses Paid/to be paid

EPISODE 2 THE SC1

It came as a complete surprise to Downes that the Bank was considering withdrawing the £300,000 loan it had advanced five years ago. To keep the loan Downes would have to supply the Bank with details of convincing development projects, before he was in a position to do so. Immediately after the meeting with the Bank, Downes called at Malone's home and told him to look into the question of suitable projects and report back to him as quickly as possible. Malone promised that there would be a report on his desk the following Monday.

The following morning Malone asked Evans and Orpenshaw to come to his office to review all the development projects Bellcrest had undertaken in the last five years and consider which project should be given priority. It very soon became clear that Evans wasn't in favour of any of the projects. Although the projects were good in themselves, he felt that from a sales point of view there was little chance of their giving Bellcrest the edge over their competitors. It was also true, as Evans went on to say, that some of the projects had been suspended and were also well outside Bellcrest's normal field of operations. To Orpenshaw, on the other hand, there was no question which project to support. It was obvious that the SC1 was the one to back. The SC1 was a speed control mechanism for vehicles driven by electricity, such as electric vans and fork-lift trucks. There are considerable advantages in using such a device, but it had been decided to suspend the SC1 five years ago, a decision that had led directly to the resignation of Donald Williams.

Malone realized that it would be extremely difficult to revive the SC1. Despite its technical advantages, there was no established market for it, and it had not been fully developed before its suspension. Malone worked on the SC1 files all weekend, having instructed Evans and Orpenshaw to meet him again the following Monday.

At the second meeting, Evans was still very much against the SC1, whereas Orpenshaw was whole-heartedly in favour of it. Five years ago the arguments against the SC1 were primarily that there were poor prospects for sales in the industrial vehicle sector and that it would have taken five years for Bellcrest to break even and longer to show a profit. It had not been clear at the time whether a market existed among car manufacturers and an added consideration was Bellcrest's lack of experience in the automotive field. There had also been the bad cost price ratio to take into account.

Malone was quick to realize that these arguments no longer held water. It was possible that with everyone wanting to get rid of pollution there already was a potential market for the SC1 in the private vehicle sector. Moreover, the prospects in the industrial vehicle sector had improved. Production costs could be cut, as Orpenshaw could easily design-in new components that would be cheaper and more efficient.

Eventually it was decided to submit the SC1 to Downes as a project deserving priority. Despite its being controversial, Malone was convinced he had taken everything into consideration and was in a position to support his choice of the SC1 with solid arguments.

Downes' immediate reaction on seeing Malone's report was to call in the Company Secretary, Charles Spence. Spence was immediately against the SC1 because of the expense involved in developing it, although he admitted it was a fine technical achievement. Despite Malone's offering to answer his questions, Spence remained highly sceptical of the SC1. Malone mentioned that his department had enough money for a market study. Downes refused to commit himself, and Malone was left to wait for his decision.

UNIT SUMMARY

Structures

The structures dealt with in this unit are:

1 Adjectives v. Adverbs:

The design is *good.*

He works very *efficiently.*

2 There is/It is:

There is no reason for cancelling the project.

It has been decided to cancel the project.

3 Verbs followed by an Infinitive (with or without an object):

Malone *asked her to get* Driver on the line.

He *wanted to revive* the SC1.

Vocabulary

The areas of vocabulary dealt with in this unit are:

1 Consideration/decision/proposal

2 Resign/dismiss

dditional Notes

Exercise E

It is not necessary for students to set out detailed information in their letters.

COMPREHENSION QUESTIONS

1 What was the Bank considering?
2 What was Downes' reaction to this?
3 Why did this put Downes in a difficult position?
4 Why did he call at Malone's home?
5 When did he want him to report back?
6 What promise did Malone make?
7 Why did Malone want to see Evans and Orpenshaw?
8 What did Malone want to know?
9 What was Evans' opinion of the development projects?
10 What was the disadvantage from a sales point of view?
11 What other disadvantages were there?
12 What was Orpenshaw's opinion?
13 What kinds of vehicles could use the SC1?
14 What happened to the project five years ago?
15 What did Malone realize?
16 Why would it be difficult to revive the SC1?
17 What were the two opposing points of view on the project?
18 Why was the SC1 suspended five years ago?
19 What other considerations had been taken into account?
20 In what way had the position changed since then?
21 Why was there a potential market for the SC1?
22 What improvements could now be made?
23 Why did Malone feel confident about his choice of the SC1?
24 What was the main problem in Spence's view?
25 What steps did Malone take to convince him?
26 Did he succeed?
27 What was Downes' reaction to the discussion?

EXERCISES

Exercise A **Complete the following sentences:**

1 Downes, Spence and Malone met to d. the threatened withdrawal of the loan. A p. to revive the SC1 was put forward. A number of important points had to be t. into a. before a d. could be reached. Malone was in f. of the SC1 but Spence was very much a. it and raised several o. Spence and Malone had an a. over the advantages and d. of the SC1 and it was clear that the matter was going to need careful c. In the end, Downes a. to keep an open mind on the SC1.

2 Five years ago the SC1 was s. . Williams, who was in charge of the project, felt that it was being a. and left the company. Nobody was quite sure if he had r. or been d.

Exercise B *These are the notes Malone made while discussing the SC1 project with Orpenshaw and Evans. Later he he had to write up these notes into a report.* **Write the sentences for him as in these examples:**

. . . . . lot of development work/still/do.
THERE WILL BE A LOT OF DEVELOPMENT WORK STILL TO DO.
. . . . . obvious/prospects/improve.
IT IS OBVIOUS THAT PROSPECTS WILL IMPROVE.

1 . . . . . sharp competition/other companies.
2 . . . . . likely to strain/production resources.
3 . . . . . a period/don't show a profit.
4 . . . . . many people/think/project/too ambitious.
5 . . . . . expanding market/automotive field.
6 . . . . . big increase/use of electric vehicles/next five years.
7 . . . . . true/must make/careful market study.
8 . . . . . possible/reduce production costs/designing-in cheaper components.
9 . . . . . good sales opportunities/variable speed control mechanism.
10 . . . . . enough money in the budget/market study.

Exercise C **Report this Dialogue. Choose the best verb from this list:**
decide/tell/want/offer/remind/advise/agree/promise/arrange/ask.

Example: *Jean, get Orpenshaw on the phone.*
Malone told Jean to get Orpenshaw on the phone.

Malone: Jean, get Orpenshaw on the phone.
Orpenshaw? Would you mind coming up to my office straight away? I want todiscuss development projects.

Orpenshaw: I'll bring all the files, shall I?

Malone: Yes. Oh, and don't forget to bring the results of the market study on the BX3.

Later in Malone's office.

Malone:	You'd better put all that in writing, Bob.
Orpenshaw:	O.K. I'll write a full report.
Malone:	I'd like you to give it to Evans by the end of the week.
Orpenshaw:	I'll definitely have it ready by Thursday.
Malone:	Well, we'll meet again on Friday morning. Could you be here at 10? Jean, put that in my diary.

Exercise D **Choose the most appropriate word from this list:**

suitable/ly	potential/ly	private/ly
technical/ly	doubtful/ly	immediate/ly
useful/ly	whole-hearted/ly	high/ly
efficient/ly	primary/ly	normal/ly

I know that the SC1 has Malone's ____ support, but I must say, Maurice. I feel ____ about the whole project. Of course the design of the SC1 is ____ advanced, but Bellcrest has no ____ experience of selling to the ____ vehicle sector. This is a ____ competitive field and my big fear is that we may not be able to produce the goods as ____ as our rivals. It might be difficult for us to take advantage of the ____ market. I am ____ concerned with the cost of this project. Production costs for the SC1 would be ____ so we cannot expect an ____ profit. I think the BX3 project would be much more ____

Exercise E **Written Task**

Answer this letter:

The Morford Vehicles Co. Ltd.,
Lagos,
Nigeria.

17th October, 19 . . .

The Sales Manager,
Bellcrest Ltd.,
Leicester,
England.

Dear Sir,

We have seen your advertisement in 'The Motor Mechanic' and are interested in electronic components for the industrial vehicle sector.

Please send detailed specifications of the BX3, quoting your price C.I.F. Lagos and stating terms of payment, discounts for regular purchases and delivery dates.

As we have considerable requirements in this field, could you please also send us a catalogue.

Yours faithfully,

James White
(Chief Buyer)

DRILLS

Drill 1 *Paul Malone and Charles Spence are arguing about what happened five years ago when the SC1 was suspended.*

Look, we decided to abandon the SC1.
I'M SORRY, BUT IT WAS NEVER DECIDED TO ABANDON THE SC1.

We had a sound reason for suspending the SC1.
I'M SORRY, BUT THERE WAS NEVER A SOUND REASON FOR SUSPENDING THE SC1.

Drill 2 *Malone is answering questions put to him by an assistant.*

What sort of design is it?
IT SEEMS TO ME IT'S RATHER GOOD.

How fast does he work?
IT SEEMS TO ME HE WORKS RATHER QUICKLY.

1 Good/well
2 Quick/quickly

3 Keen/keenly
4 Bad/badly
5 Efficient/efficiently
6 Slow/slowly
7 Good/well
8 Enthusiastic/enthusiastically
9 Urgent/urgently
10 Uncertain/uncertainly

Dialogue Opening a meeting

Paul Malone is opening a meeting at which he will be chairman.

Good morning, gentlemen. Please sit down.
Are we all here?
Let's make a start then, shall we?
Now, you've all had a copy of the agenda, haven't you?
Right, let's get down to business.
Can we deal with that under Any Other Business?
Yes. Charles, would you care to comment on that?

Drill 3 *Paul Malone is discussing the SC1 with Evans and Orpenshaw.*

Evans: Well, it seems obvious that we've got to carry out a Market Survey.

Malone: AS I SEE IT, THE THING WE'VE GOT TO CONSIDER IS *WHEN* TO CARRY OUT A MARKET SURVEY.

1 When?	3 How?	5 When?	7 How?
2 Where?	4 How?	6 When?	8 When?

Drill 4 *a) Malone, Evans and Orpenshaw are still discussing the SC1. Unfortunately, Orpenshaw doesn't agree with the ideas of the other two.*

Evans: My feeling is that we should review *all* the projects before going into details.

Orpenshaw: WOULDN'T IT BE BETTER TO GO INTO DETAILS FIRST?

b) Orpenshaw is rather rude when he disagrees in that way with his colleagues. Listen to him now, when is he being more polite:

Evans: My feeling is that we should review *all* the projects before going into details.

Orpenshaw: FORGIVE ME, BUT WOULDN'T IT BE BETTER TO GO INTO DETAILS FIRST?

c) Sometimes you may want to use another phrase, instead of 'Forgive me, but . . .':

Evans: The best thing would be to select a project and then discuss it with Downes.

Orpenshaw YOU MAY HAVE A POINT THERE, BUT WOULDN'T IT BE BETTER TO DISCUSS IT WITH DOWNES FIRST?

ACTIVE LISTENING

Tom Driver is Bellcrest's Production Manager, He is discussing the news that the SC1 may be revived with Malone's assistant.

1 How did Driver find out about the SC1?

2 How did Malone's assistant find out about it?

3 Is the project secret or has the company told its employees about it?

4 How do they think this information became known?

5 What is Driver's general attitude to the possible revival of the SC1?

6 What does he think Downes' attitude will be?

7 Do the two men think there is a lot of support for the project?

8 What do they think about the market for the SC1?

9 What is Spence's reputation?

10 Does Driver agree with Spence's position on the SC1?

What do you understand by the following expressions:

1 We thought it was completely hush-hush at this stage.

2 This has really been his baby ever since then.

. . . .

. . . .

3 It might give us the edge over our competitors.

. . . .

. . . .

4 It's rather a step into the dark, isn't it?

. . . .

. . . .

5 You know what a tight-fisted old so-and-so he is.

. . . .

. . . .

6 With him it's like getting blood out of a stone.

. . . .

. . . .

ROLE SIMULATION

Statement of Problem

At one point during the course of discussions at Bellcrest as to whether to take up development of the SC1 again, Malone decided to call all interested parties together to a meeting. The purpose of the meeting was to come to a firm decision as to whether or not to develop the SC1. Those present at the meeting were Malone and his assistant, Spence and his assistant, Orpenshaw and his assistant, Evans, Driver and his assistant, and the Head of the Market Research department.

You should re-enact this meeting. The purpose of it is to come to your own decision, as if you were representing Bellcrest Ltd., as to whether to submit the SC1 to Downes as a development project deserving top priority or not.

The letters SC1 stand for AC Variable Speed Control, Mark 1. It is a speed control mechanism for vehicles driven by electricity, such as electric vans. Up till now these vehicles have worked off batteries, but the batteries are big and heavy, and can store only a limited amount of electrical power. They have to be recharged frequently. A fork-lift truck, for example, keeps stopping and starting. Every time it changes speed, it demands more power from its engine. Every time this demand changes, a lot of power – in the form of direct current from the battery – is lost. By changing the direct current into alternating current the SC1 would save a lot of power.

Written follow-up

Write up the minutes of the meeting.

DESCRIPTION OF ROLES

Paul Malone, Marketing Manager

You are the Chairman of the meeting, and must therefore draw up an agenda before the meeting. The purpose of the meeting is for you to hear the views of all those present on the SC1. During the course of the meeting you must guide the discussion along the lines you want. You must also see to it that a decision is reached on whether to submit the SC1 to Downes as a development project or not. Outwardly you are neutral in that you do not give the impression of having already made up your mind. Inwardly, you are determined to persuade those present to support the SC1. You have an assistant, James Jackson, to whom you can delegate.

James Jackson, Assistant to the Marketing Manager

You are Paul Malone's assistant, and it is therefore your job to assist him in running the meeting. You are very much in favour of the SC1, and should prepare arguments to support its development.

Charles Spence, Company Secretary

You are very much against the SC1, and should prepare arguments against its development. You were against the SC1 five years ago on the grounds of the expense involved in its development and the lack of a market for it. A lot of money was wasted in the past on the SC1, and you are concerned not to let it happen again. You have an assistant, Duncan Warburton.

Duncan Warburton, Assistant to the Company Secretary

You follow Charles Spence's lead in opposing the SC1. You should prepare arguments against it and support Charles Spence, unless you can be convinced otherwise.

Bob Orpenshaw, Head of Research and Development
You are fanatically in favour of the SC1. It is technically a brilliant invention and you know it. It is the most interesting project you have ever worked on. You should prepare arguments in favour of development of the SC1. You have an assistant, Peter Thurrock.

Peter Thurrock, Assistant to Bob Orpenshaw
You are Bob Orpenshaw's assistant, and are neutral as regards the SC1. You agree with Orpenshaw that the SC1 is an interesting project, but are not convinced that it is the best project. You should prepare and propose an alternative project, which you yourself invented, such as your potentially very successful RX1, an electronic component in great demand in the aircraft industry. You hate Dennis Evans.

Dennis Evans, Sales Manager
You are frightened of supporting the SC1 for fear of losing your job. You remember Donald Williams only too well. You are therefore neutral, waiting to see what the others will say before committing yourself.

Tom Driver, Production Manager
At the meeting you will certainly be asked whether there would be any difficulties in producing the SC1, and should prepare for this. You have an assistant, Harold Thwaites, to help you. As far as the SC1 itself is concerned you are neutral, but you can foresee difficulties in production as it is a product outside Bellcrest's normal range.

Harold Thwaites, Assistant to the Production Manager
Your job is to assist Tom Driver. Like him, you foresee production difficulties with the SC1. You should be prepared to explain exactly what these difficulties would be. You hate Bob Orpenshaw.

Henry Wall, Head of Market Research
You are by nature a cautious man, and are particularly cautious about the SC1. Your informal survey indicates that there is a potential market for such a device both in the industrial and in the private vehicle sectors, but the market would have to be developed, and this would cost money. At the meeting you should be prepared to give such details of your survey as are necessary.

EPISODE 3. MEETINGS

Malone submitted his report to Downes, in which he strongly recommended that the SC1 should be given priority over other development projects. Downes did not commit himself, but called a management meeting to discuss the report.

Downes opened the meeting by summarizing the position Bellcrest was in. He mentioned that Ashburnham's Bank had suggested that Bellcrest should repay the £300,000 loan made five years previously, unless the company needed the money to finance new developments. This move by the Bank meant that Malone had had to finalize his proposals for product development somewhat earlier than Downes had originally intended. He went on to invite the comments of those present on Malone's report.

Driver, as Production Manager, pointed out that producing the SC1. would be far from easy. Several products were being run down, however, and by adapting existing machinery some spare production capacity could be gained in the factory. He suggested that if Bellcrest wanted to introduce a new product line, they should start planning for it at once, as it was a suitable time to do this.

Spence accepted Driver's point about launching a new product line at the most suitable time, but questioned whether the SC1. was the most suitable product. He pointed out that Malone was recommending that they should revive a project that had been suspended by the Board five years previously. The Board would be unlikely to view its return favourably. He also wondered whether Malone was recommending that they should abandon current projects, on which a great deal of money had been spent over the last two years, in favour of the SC1, and went on to raise further objections on the grounds of expense and the uncertainty of the market.

Despite Spence's constant objections, Malone was able to defend the SC1 and gain the support of the meeting for the project. Although at the end of the meeting Spence still had reservations, Malone succeeded in getting a general agreement that new product development should be centred on the SC1. After the meeting, Downes warned Malone in private that the blame for any failure of the SC1 project would rest on his shoulders. He also stressed the need for absolute security.

As soon as he had management support Malone started work on getting the SC1 project off the ground. In consultation with Evans he decided to call in a firm of management consultants, M.P. Consultants, to carry out a market survey. He also suggested that they should engage a product executive who would be solely responsible for marketing the SC1. He recommended that they should approach Alan Beeston, who had had dealings with Bellcrest when he worked for the Ministry of Defence and was now looking for a job.

The decision taken at the management meeting was an important one for Bellcrest. Equally important was a chance meeting in an aeroplane over the Atlantic between Donald Williams, formerly Marketing Manager of Bellcrest, and now Managing Director of Electrovans, and Sam Urwin, Executive Vice-President of Passlee Electronics, a Canadian corporation and one of Bellcrest's largest overseas customers.

Urwin was on his way to Bellcrest, and Williams suggested that he should also visit Electrovans to have a look at their vehicle components, as to the best of his knowledge Bellcrest was not involved in the automotive field. When, after his arrival in England, Urwin mentioned this invitation to Downes and Malone during a game of golf, he was surprised at their obvious concern.

UNIT SUMMARY

Structures The structures dealt with in this unit are:

1 Used to/be used to/use:

They *used to* do business with Bellcrest.
They *are used to* exporting components.
The SC1 *is used* in electric vehicles.

2 The Gerund as a Noun:

Exporting can be a risky business.

3 Must/mustn't/needn't:

You *mustn't* be late for work.
You *needn't* attend the meeting.

4 Should/would:

He suggested that we *should* back the SC1.
Production of the SC1 *would* not be easy.

Vocabulary The areas of vocabulary dealt with in this unit are:

1 Cost/expenditure
2 Production
3 Market Studies.

Additional Notes Summary

There are a number of logical connectives, such as 'although' and 'despite' in the summary. Do not treat these now, as connectives are taken up in detail in later Episodes.

Exercise C

This is a two phase oral exercise: in the first phase the pupils are invited to make a single sentence:

e.g. 'Introducing the new product line is going to be expensive'.

In the second phase the pupil's statement is confirmed by a second pupil:

e.g. 'Introducing the new product line is going to be expensive'.
'Introducing a new product line is always expensive'.

Dialogue

Closing a meeting and Drill 4

You should encourage your pupils to use the formulae practised in the dialogue and drill four in the role-play.

Role Simulation

The problem is similar to that encountered in Episode 2, though viewed from a different angle. Emphasize the difference in language required between the informal meeting of Episode 2, and the formal management meeting they are asked to re-enact here.

COMPREHENSION QUESTIONS

1 What did Malone recommend in his report to Downes?
2 What did Downes think they should do about this?
3 What had Ashburnham's Bank suggested?
4 Why did Malone have to write his report so quickly?
5 What did Driver think would be a difficult job?
6 Would it be possible to use existing machinery for producing the SC1?
7 What did Driver think they should do about planning?
8 Which of Driver's points did Spence accept?
9 What did he think about the suitability of the SC1 in general?
10 How did Spence think the Board would see Malone's recommendation?
11 Why was Spence against abandoning current development projects?
12 What did Spence think about the cost of developing the SC1?
13 Did he think there was a market for the product?
14 What agreement was reached about new product development?
15 Did Spence support the decision?
16 What was the warning Downes gave to Malone afterwards?
17 What did Malone start work on after gaining management support?
18 Who are M.P. Consultants?
19 Why did Malone and Evans decide to call them in?
20 What new post did Malone suggest they should create?
21 What would the new employee do?
22 Who did he recommend they should approach?
23 How did Malone know about him?
24 Who is Donald Williams?
25 Who did he used to work for?
26 Where did he meet Urwin?
27 Had Urwin and Williams arranged to meet on the plane?
28 What was the connection between Passlee Electronics and Bellcrest?
29 Why was Urwin going to England?
30 What did Williams suggest Urwin should do?
31 Did he want to compete with Bellcrest?
32 Why were Downes and Malone concerned about Williams' invitation to Urwin?

EXERCISES

Exercise A **Complete the following sentences:**

1 Malone wanted to be quite sure that there was a p. market for the SC1, so he decided to c. a market s. . He called in a firm of m. c. who were s. in marketing.

2 Some time ago Bellcrest invested a considerable amount in new buildings and machinery, so their p. f. are now first-class. However, a new p. l. like the SC1 would put a strain on their p. r. . It was necessary to plan immediately so that the p. c. of their factory could be increased. Bellcrest still had many p. l. which had not yet reached the end of their l. c.

3 The amount of money a company sells its products for is the *price* of the product. A company *prices* its products carefully.
What a company pays for materials or labour is the *cost* of materials or the *cost* of labour.
When a company *costs* a product, it decides how much money it will need to develop, produce and market the product.
If the company gets back in sales as much as it spends, then it *covers its costs.*
If a project is too *expensive*, the company abandons it, because it means too much *expense.*
The total amount of money paid out each year by a company is the annual *expenditure.*
When a businessman pays money to travel for his company, he can claim travel *expenses.*

a Development of the BX10 was stopped because it was too
b We'll have to buy the BX13 from Bellcrest although it's rather high.
c Spence opposed the SC1 on the grounds of
d Do you know the of raw materials?
e Our on marketing has increased over the last year.
f We had to make price increases because of the of labour.
g We can't spend so much on development if we're going to our

h The manufacturers won't buy these components if the is too high.
i After taking a visitor from Electrovans out to lunch, Mr Malone claimed from Bellcrest.
j We'll have to the development of this product line very carefully.

Exercise B **Make sentences from these notes:**

Example: *Bellcrest/complete/in the electronics field.*
Bellcrest is used to competing in the electronics field.

1 Bellcrest's Sales Manager/work/for Davidson's before.

2 An experienced salesman/deal with/awkward questions.
3 Our Managing Director/be/against this project.
4 This mechanism/control/the speed of the vehicle.
5 M.P. Consultants/prepare/market surveys in the automotive field.
6 Sometimes a bank loan/finance/new production facilities.
7 Beverman and Jones/export/components to Germany ten years ago.
8 Fork-lift trucks/carry/the goods to the store.
9 Malone/submit/reports to Downes/by now.
10 Modern production lines/increase/production capacity.

Exercise C Make sentences from the table below:

Example: a) *Abandoning the research project is going to waste money.*
b) *Yes. Abandoning a research project always wastes money.*

introduce finance abandon suspend sell	the	new product line research project machinery development plan	is going to	be expensive increase profits save money be difficult waste money

Exercise D Fill in the blanks using should/shouldn't/would/wouldn't:

Malone: Right, Dennis, let's get down to business. Now what about this market study? Which of the management consultant firms ______ we go to?

Evans: Management consultants? Is that really necessary? ______ it be possible to do that ourselves?

Malone: Oh, no, Dennis. This job is far too big for us. It ______ be done by an outside firm. It ______ do to make any mistakes, ______ it?

Evans: Well, in that case I think M.P. Consultants ______ be the best people to go to. After all, they're specialists in marketing, so they ______ be able to answer all our questions.

Malone: How long ______ we give them to complete the study?

Evans: Well, that rather depends on how soon we want it. It ______ take them long. They're very efficient. They ______ manage to get it done by the end of the month. I think my assistant ______ go and see them in person. The chief consultant is a friend of his. If he explained the position, they ______ probably give it priority.

Exercise E **Written task**

Williams met Sam Urwin on the plane. In the hope that Passlee Electronics would eventually do business with Electrovans, Williams wrote a follow-up letter to Urwin. Write this letter for him. Use these notes:

it was most pleasant
feel sure you will be interested
hope you will be able to visit
Tuesday 29th
offer him dinner

DRILLS

Drill 1 *Bellcrest's Personnel Manger is answering a recruit's questions about his new job.*

Do I have to write a report every day?
NO, YOU NEEDN'T WRITE A REPORT EVERY DAY.

What happens if I file documents in the wrong place?
YOU MUSTN'T FILE DOCUMENTS IN THE WRONG PLACE ON ANY ACCOUNT.

Drill 2 *Malone has met an old friend of his, and they are talking about Bellcrest's work.*

Do you make components for electric motors now?
NO, WE USED TO MAKE THEM.

Don't you find it difficult to work with transistors?
NO, WE'RE USED TO WORKING WITH THEM.

(You must choose which is the better answer – for example, 'We used to make them' or 'we're used to making them'.)

Dialogue Closing a meeting

After listening to everybody's opinions on the SC1 project, Downes closes the meeting.

I see. Now you've all had your say. Has anyone anything further they wish to raise?

Good. Are we all in favour of Malone's proposal?

What about you, Charles?

With reservations, but in favour. Minute that, please, Miss Armstrong.

The next meeting will be at the same time next week. Is that all right?

Now, is there any other business?

Good. In that case, I declare the meeting closed.

Drill 3 *Spence agreed to support the SC1, but with reservations. He is discussing his reservations with Paul Malone.*

Listen Charles. I'm sure the answer to our problems is diversification.
YES, THERE'S CERTAINLY A CASE FOR DIVERSIFICATION, ALTHOUGH IT'S A MAJOR CHANGE OF POLICY.

I still think we should revive the SC1.
YES, THERE'S CERTAINLY A CASE FOR REVIVING THE SC1, ALTHOUGH IT'S NOT IN OUR FIELD.

1 Major change of policy
2 Not in our field
3 Take time
4 Expensive
5 A waste of money
6 Cost a great deal
7 Too early yet
8 Difficult to persuade the Board

Drill 4 *Maurice Downes is Chairman of the Management Committee. One of a Chairman's important functions is to control the meeting, and keep to the correct order of business.*

Mr Chairman – I feel it's time we discussed costs.

BEFORE WE DISCUSS COSTS, MAY I DRAW YOUR ATTENTION TO PARAGRAPH 3 OF THE REPORT?

A good Chairman, when he guides a meeting in this way, lets the speaker know that he won't forget the point that was raised.

BEFORE WE DISCUSS COSTS, MAY I DRAW YOUR ATTENTION TO PARAGRAPH 3 OF THE REPORT? PERHAPS WE COULD RETURN TO THE QUESTION OF COSTS LATER?

1 paragraph 3 of the report
2 another point
3 the next point on the agenda

4 another important matter
5 the sales reports
6 this letter from the Bank
7 something we've overlooked
8 lunch arrangements.

ACTIVE LISTENING

Malone and his assistants have just returned from a meeting of the Management Committee and are discussing the SC1 project.

1 Why was it necessary to start planning immediately?

. . . .

. . . .

2 What will Orpenshaw's reaction to the decision be?

. . . .

. . . .

3 What is Orpenshaw planning to do?

. . . .

. . . .

4 Why does Malone think they should commission a market survey and what does he hope to get from it?

. . . .

. . . .

5 What disadvantage does his assistant point out?

. . . .

. . . .

6 How will the survey be financed?

. . . .

. . . .

7 Why might Dennis Evans be hurt if Malone approaches a firm of Management Consultants?

. . . .

. . . .

8 What does Malone propose to do so that Evans will not be hurt?

. . . .

. . . .

9 Which other problem do they discuss?

. . . .

. . . .

10 What does Malone want to do?

. . . .

. . . .

11 Why does he feel this is necessary?

. . . .

. . . .

12 Why does Malone think Alan Beeston is a suitable candidate for this post?

. . . .

. . . .

ROLE SIMULATION

Statement of Problem

After Malone had gained the support of Evans and Orpenshaw for the SC1, he still had to submit his proposal to Downes. Downes decided to call a meeting at management level to reach a formal decision as to whether to proceed with the SC1 or not. He invited Dennis Evans and Bob Orpenshaw to attend, in view of their involvement with the SC1.

The problem to be solved is whether to submit the SC1 to the Board of Directors as a priority for new product development. At management level there are further considerations to be taken into account, such as possible alternatives to the SC1, potential markets both at home and abroad, the Board's possible reaction to the proposal, the expense involved and the existence of competition. At this level, the SC1 project also raises matters of company policy, such as the question of whether Bellcrest should stick to its present field of operations or move outside this field to open up new ranges of products.

Written follow-up

Write a short report on the meeting, explaining the arguments for and against the SC1 and what decision was reached.

DESCRIPTION OF ROLES

Maurice Downes

You are the chairman of the meeting, and must therefore guide the discussion towards a decision while letting everybody have their say. You are not willing to give your own opinion on the SC1 project until you have heard everybody's views. As chairman you are responsible for organizing the meeting. You have a personal assistant and a secretary. At the end of the meeting, ask your secretary to give a summary of the discussion.

Paul Malone

Your purpose at the meeting is to get the support of those present for the SC1 project. You must fight for the SC1 all the way against any opposition. You should, therefore, prepare as many arguments as possible in favour of your project.

Charles Spence

You are very much against the SC1 and are determined to stop the project. You should therefore prepare as many arguments as possible against the SC1.

Tom Driver

You are neutral as far as the SC1 is concerned. You should be ready to be convinced either way. You should be prepared to answer questions about Bellcrest's ability to actually produce the SC1, and should invent such statistics as you feel to be necessary to do this.

David Smithson

You are the Personnel Manager. As far as the SC1 is concerned you have an open mind. You are worried, however, about the possible consequences of introducing a new type of product, as you feel this may involve additional training of employees and you don't have the money in your budget to do this. You should therefore question Malone carefully about whether additional training either of salesmen or of the men on the shop floor will be necessary.

Bob Orpenshaw

You are naturally in favour of the SC1 and cannot understand anyone being against it. You are rude to anyone who opposes the project, and you hate Charles Spence. You should be prepared to elaborate on what a brilliant technical achievement the SC1 is.

Dennis Evans

You are very anxious to say the right thing, and agree with whatever Downes says. Privately you are in favour of the SC1, particulary as your sales force have indicated that they have heard that potential customers would be interested in such a device.

William Jenkins

You are head of the Overseas Sales Department. You are very interested in the SC1 , as your contacts in Europe have indicated that there is a need for such a device. You are cautious about committing yourself to the SC1 too quickly, but are quite ready to be convinced by good arguments.

Henry Pollard

You are Downes' Personal Assistant. Your main job is therefore to assist Downes run the meeting. You should be prepared to calm anyone down who gets too excited at the meeting. You are particularly anxious to see that nobody gets upset. You don't care one way or the other about the SC1.

Miss Armstrong

Your job is to keep the minutes of the meeting. You may well be asked to give a summary at the end of the meeting.

JOBS

Malone finds that getting the SC1 project under way is not going to be easy. The first setback occurs during his game of golf with Downes and Urwin. Urwin mentions that he is visiting Electrovans to have a look at their vehicle components. Now Malone has a problem. If he tells Urwin that Bellcrest is moving into the field of vehicle components, he will risk Electrovans getting to hear about the SC1. On the other hand if he doesn't tell Urwin that Bellcrest has plans to develop the SC1, Urwin will probably commit Passlee Electronics to buying from a competitor. Downes settles the matter by telling Malone not to reveal his plans yet.

A further complication arises the following day. Evans has seen Orpenshaw in the canteen and has just heard that Orpenshaw has been offered another job. Malone is extremely concerned about this, and immediately gets in touch with Orpenshaw, as he fully realizes that if Orpenshaw leaves Bellcrest there will be no chance of developing the SC1.

When Malone meets Orpenshaw he tries to find out who has approached him, but can get no more out of him than Evans did. Orpenshaw simply answers that he hasn't yet made up his mind about the job, and that he doesn't want to talk about it. He says he won't accept less money than he's getting at Bellcrest. Malone then reminds him of his importance to the SC1 project, but Orpenshaw merely points out it was his invention.

Unable to get a definite answer out of Orpenshaw, Malone takes the problem to Downes. Downes takes the news calmly and suggests that Malone should check up on the terms of Orpenshaw's contract of employment. He accepts the fact that if Orpenshaw leaves, that will be the end of the SC1 project. Malone suggests that it is Donald Williams who is trying to get Orpenshaw away from Bellcrest, but Downes thinks that it is more likely to be Urwin.

Malone has better luck when he interviews Alan Beeston. Beeston used to work for the Ministry of Defence and as he was then involved in negotiating contracts for electronic equipment for the army, he is used to dealing with the type of products that Bellcrest manufactures. Although he doesn't actually say so, Malone has Beeston in mind for the new post of Product Executive for the SC1. During the course of the interview it becomes more and more apparent that Beeston would be suitable for this post. He has had experience with electronic equipment while working for the Ministry, although he has only been involved in the buying side. At present he is working for Beamish Motors, and so has already gained some experience of the business world in general and the car industry in particular – an important point in Malone's eyes.

Later the same week Malone and Evans visit M.P. Consultants, the firm who are doing the market study for Bellcrest. Although the brief was clear, Dr Perkins wants to go over the terms of reference in more detail. Malone confirms that the three main areas in which Bellcrest are interested are industrial vehicles, commercial vehicles and small electric cars for use in cities. M.P. Consultants have just completed a survey on the use of cars in cities, and if Malone is interested, they will try to get permission for Bellcrest to have access to some of the data.

To Malone's surprise, he finds that M.P. Consultants have already been approached by another company interested in a market survey for a product similar to the SC1. In view of this unexpected news, Malone is even more anxious for a preliminary study of the market in the United Kingdom to be ready in four weeks' time. The existence of rivals to the SC1 is a possibility Malone had not anticipated.

UNIT SUMMARY

Structures The structures dealt with in this unit are:

1 Conditionals:

a Present Tenses:
If Orpenshaw *goes,* Bellcrest *won't be able to* develop the SC1.

b Present Tense and Modal 'Should':
If *you're interested,* then you *should contact* our Sales Manager.

2 Present Simple contrasted with Present Continuous:

Bellcrest *manufacture* electronic components.
Bellcrest *are working on* a new AC speed control device.

3 Present Perfect and Position of Adverbs of Frequency:

We *have already commissioned* a market study.
We *haven't heard* the results *yet.*

Vocabulary The areas of vocabulary dealt with in this unit are:

1 promotion, vacancy, contract, employment.
2 licensing agreement, negotiate, terms etc.
3 survey, terms of reference, brief, data etc.

Additional Notes **The Summary** – The summary is written with a present time reference in order to demonstrate the contrasts between the tenses dealt with in this unit.

Exercise C – This exercise contrasts Present Simple and Present Continuous.

Role Simulation – The Statement of Problem contains a number of words that will probably be unknown to the pupils. The teacher should therefore take appropriate steps to introduce the vocabulary and fix it in his pupils' minds before requiring them to act out the situation.

COMPREHENSION QUESTIONS

1 How easy does Malone find work on the new project?
2 Where does he learn about Urwin's interest in vehicle components?
3 Why doesn't he tell Urwin about the SC1?
4 Is there also a risk in not telling him?
5 How does Malone solve this problem?
6 Where does he go after the game?
7 How long has Evans known about the offer to Orpenshaw when he speaks to Malone?
8 Where did Orpenshaw tell him this?
9 Was Orpenshaw expecting the offer?
10 Why is Malone concerned about the matter?
11 What decision does Orpenshaw say he has reached about the offer?
12 Does Orpenshaw want more money in his new job?
13 Does Malone try to make him stay?
14 What does Orpenshaw say about the SC1?

15 What does Malone do about Orpenshaw?
16 Is Downes angry when he hears about the matter?
17 What does he suggest to Malone?
18 Does he think they can develop the project without Orpenshaw?
19 Where does Malone think the offer to Orpenshaw has come from?
20 Does Downes agree?
21 Why does Malone interview Beeston?
22 Who did Beeston used to work for?
23 How much does he know about the type of product Bellcrest manufactures?
24 What does Malone tell him about the new post?
25 What does Malone think about his suitability for the post?
26 Has Beeston had experience of both buying and selling electronic equipment?
27 What did Bellcrest ask M.P. Consultants to do?
28 Why do Malone and Evans visit them?
29 What are Bellcrest's main areas of interest?
30 When did M.P. Consultants complete their survey on cars in cities?
31 Will they get permission for Bellcrest to see the survey?
32 What does Malone learn from Dr Perkins that surprises him?
33 What does he do about this?
34 Why does he want the study so quickly?

EXERCISES

Exercise A **Complete the following sentences:**

1 Beeston left the Ministry of Defence because there seemed to be little p. of ever rising to a higher position. He had been there for five years and had not been p. . Beamish Motors had several v. to f. and they o. him a j. at a high salary, with good p. for p. . After he had signed the c. of e. he found out that he was stuck behind a desk all day doing boring routine paperwork. He wanted more j. s. so he asked the management if he could t. to one of their subsidiary companies.

2 Urwin came over from Canada to re-negotiate the l. a. between Passlee Electronics and Bellcrest. Under the t. of this a. Passlee is allowed to manufacture Bellcrest products in Canada. This does not, however, prevent them from n. c. with other companies.

3 Bellcrest commissioned M.P. Consultants to conduct a preliminary s. on the market prospects of the SC1. Their instructions were laid down in the b. that Malone sent to Dr Perkins. Their t. of r. included industrial vehicles, commercial vehicles, and electrically driven private vehicles. These were the three a. that interested Bellcrest and they asked the consultants to organize their report under these h. The company had already gathered some facts on the use of cars in cities and they offered to give Bellcrest the d. . As Bellcrest did not want anyone to know about their revived interest in the SC1, they asked the consultants to t. the matter as c.

Exercise B **Join the two phrases to make a sentence using 'if':**

Examples:
Orpenshaw resigning.
Williams offering him a job.

If Orpenshaw resigns, Williams will offer him a job.

The Bank withdrawing the loan.
Bellcrest not developing a new project.

The Bank will withdraw the loan if Bellcrest doesn't develop a new project.

1 Urwin visiting Electrovans.
Urwin enquiring about vehicle components.

2 Electrovans hearing about the SC1.
Malone informing Urwin.

3 Malone not informing Urwin.
Passlee Electronics buying from a competitor.

4 Electrovans competing with Bellcrest.
Bellcrest entering the private vehicle sector.

5 Bellcrest needing a product executive.
Bellcrest developing the SC1.

Example:
Orpenshaw deciding to stay.
Bellcrest offering him more money.

If Orpenshaw decides to stay, Bellcrest should offer him more money.

6 Bellcrest appointing Beeston.
The Board approving the new post.

7 Bellcrest treating the project as confidential.
Other companies competing.

8 Electrovans producing a speed control mechanism.
Bellcrest examining the patents carefully.

9 Bellcrest getting finance from other sources.
The Bank refusing to renew the loan.

10 The consultants confirming their fears.
Bellcrest accepting the facts.

Exercise C Complete these sentences:

1 Malone is worried because Urwin (visit) ______ Electrovans to have a look at their vehicle components. He (not want) ______ to tell Urwin that Bellcrest (move) ______ into the field of vehicle components. But if he (not tell) ______ Urwin about the SC1, he will risk Urwin buying from Electrovans. He also (think) ______ Williams (try) ______ to get Orpenshaw away from Bellcrest. Malone (take) ______ the problem to Downes who suggests it is Urwin who (try) ______ to take Orpenshaw from Bellcrest and if he (succeed) ______ there will be no chance of developing the SC1. Downes (settle) ______ the matter by telling Malone not to inform Urwin of Bellcrest's plans.

Exercise D Complete the sentences from the notes:

Examples:
M.P. Consultants/complete/survey/use/cars in cities/(just)

M.P. Consultants have just completed a survey on the use of cars in cities.

Beeston/have/any experience/electronics industry/(ever)?

Has Beeston ever had any experience in the electronics industry?

1 Other companies/show/interest/this market/(already).
2 The Ministry of Defence/draw up/terms/the contract/(yet)?
3 We/sell/components/private vehicle sector/before/(never).
4 Orpenshaw/not decide/accept the offer/new job/(yet).
5 You/think of/changing your job/(ever)?

6 Since 1965/Bellcrest/renew/the patents/(annually).
7 There/be/any consumer demand/electrically driven cars/(never).
8 Hanson/write/series of articles/the motor industry/(just).
9 The Directors/finished/discussing Malone's report/the SC1/(almost).
10 Malone/not tell/Urwin/Bellcrest's development plans/(yet)?

Exercise E **Written Task**

After Malone had interviewed Beeston, he prepared a memorandum for Maurice Downes.

Write this memo for him. Use these notes:

B.Sc. Manchester University.
Ministry of Defence for 6 years after graduation.
Contracts for electronic equipment.
With Beamish Motors for last year.
Interested in electronics industry – good ideas.

DRILLS

Drill 1 *Bellcrest employees are discussing the SC1.*

Evans tells me that Orpenshaw is about to leave.
WELL, IF ORPENSHAW LEAVES WE WON'T BE ABLE TO DEVELOP THE SC1.

But I heard he's going to stay.
WELL, IF HE STAYS WE SHOULD BE ABLE TO DEVELOP IT.

1 develop/SC1	6 sell
2 develop	7 make/success
3 make/profit	8 make/success
4 make/profit	9 go ahead
5 sell	10 go ahead

Drill 2 *Charles Spence has arrived in his office and has a number of questions to ask his assistant.*

When is Malone starting work on the SC1?
I THINK YOU'LL FIND DOWNES HASN'T APPROVED THE PROJECT YET.

When did Malone leave for London?
I THINK YOU'LL FIND HE'S ONLY JUST LEFT.

Notes

1 Downes/approve project – not yet.
2 He/leave – only just.
3 We/send off an invoice – only just.
4 They/complete the preliminary survey – nearly.
5 They/receive our letter – never.
6 Orpenshaw/send in an estimate – not yet.
7 They/deliver on time – always.
8 They/settle the account – already.

Dialogue **Transferring a telephone call**

Paul Malone is interviewing Alan Beeston when he is interrupted by a telephone call from Dr Perkins of M.P. Consultants.

Tell her I'll ring back later, would you?

Oh very well, put her through.

Malone here.

I see. Look, I'm afraid I'm rather tied up at the moment. Would you mind speaking to my Sales Manager?

Yes, I'm sure he'll be able to answer any questions you may have.

Yes, I'm looking forward to it as well. Hold on a moment, and I'll have you transferred.

Malone here. Would you transfer this call to Mr Evans, please?

Thank you very much.

Drill 3 *Malone and Spence are discussing the appointment of a product executive. Spence thinks Malone is not considering the question carefully enough, and raises objections to what he says.*

What I'm saying is we must have a product executive.
IT'S ALL VERY WELL FOR YOU TO SAY WE MUST HAVE A PRODUCT EXECUTIVE, BUT HAVE YOU CONSIDERED THE EXPENSE?

Oh, I think we just forget the expense, don't you?
IT'S ALL VERY WELL FOR YOU TO SAY WE JUST FORGET THE EXPENSE, BUT HAVE YOU CONSIDERED THE BOARD'S REACTION?

1 The expense
2 The Board's reaction
3 His qualifications
4 His actual experience
5 An actual figure
6 Dennis Evans' position
7 Beeston's actual duties
8 In any detail

Drill 4 *Dr Mary Perkins of M.P. Consultants range Bellcrest the day before Evans and Malone went to her office in London. She spoke to Evans.*

a Hello, Dr Perkins. I hear you would like to discuss some points on the SC1 before we come to London tomorrow.
YES, I STILL DON'T UNDERSTAND *WHO* IS COMING TO LONDON TOMORROW.

b *Dr Perkins is being more polite.*
I hear you would like to discuss some points on the SC1 before we come to London tomorrow.
FORGIVE ME IF I'M BEING STUPID, BUT I STILL DON'T UNDERSTAND *WHO* IS COMING TO LONDON TOMORROW.

Notes

1 Who?
2 Why?
3 When?
4 Which?
5 What type?
6 What product?
7 When?
8 What time?

ACTIVE LISTENING

Mr Holmes, a marketing consultant, is being interviewed about the nature of his work.

1 What is the main function of a marketing consultant?

....

....

2 How does this help companies?

....

....

3 What work is involved in the launching of a new product or the redevelopment of an old one?

....

....

4 Why can't this be done by the regular staff?

....

....

5 Why is the marketing consultant only called in when a company steps outside its established field of activity?

....

....

6 Does the consultant usually get clear instructions from the company before beginning his investigations?

....

....

7 What must the consultant do first when he isn't given clear instructions.

....

....

8 What three things does the consultant consider when he defines the objectives of a company?

....

....

9 When is a questionnaire of little use?

....

....

10 When is a questionnaire relevant?

....

....

11 What problems are there as regards questionnaires?

....

....

12 What sort of people normally reply to these questionnaires?

....

....

13 How can one find out the opinions of the others?

....

....

14 What are the disadvantages of this?

....

....

ROLE SIMULATION

Statement of Problem

Up till now Bellcrest have kept the marketing, production and development departments separate from each other. Each department has had its own departmental head responsible directly to Maurice Downes as Managing Director. There have, of course, been frequent interdepartmental meetings at which the activities of each department have been co-ordinated in accordance with company policy, but there has been no overlapping of responsibility at lower levels between departments. The sales force, for example, have only been responsible for actually selling the products, and have not had to concern themselves in the least either with their development or with their production.

Now Malone has announced that he wants to appoint a product executive for the SC1, whose duty would be to plan for most of the activities affecting the profitability of the product, Such a post would naturally involve a degree of responsibility within the marketing, production and development departments, possibly within the finance department, at a lower than managerial level.

The Personnel Manager is fully aware that Malone's proposal to create the post of Product Executive for the SC1 is a controversial one. It involves a departure from standard company organization, and might well set a precedent leading to a complete reorganization of the structure of the company. Reluctant to approv Malone's proposal on his own initiative, he has called a meeting of those who would be affected by the creation of this post.

The object of the meeting therefore is to consider whether Malone's proposal is desirable in principle, to discuss what effect this would have on existing company structure and to work out the exact terms of reference the post of Product Executive would entail. The terms of reference would include, among other points, the areas of responsibility of the Product Executive within each department, to whom he would be directly responsible and for what, and what salary should be paid for such a post.

Existing Structure of Bellcrest

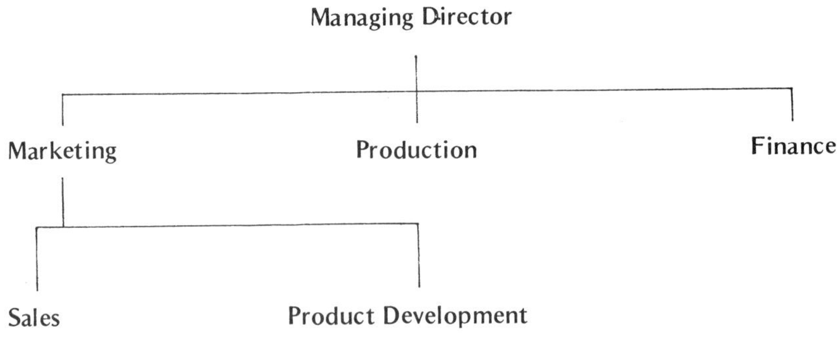

Written Task

Write a letter to a subsidiary company of Bellcrest Ltd., explaining to the Marketing Manager that a product executive for the SC1 is shortly to be appointed and defining his duties insofar as they will affect him.

DESCRIPTION OF ROLES

David Smithson

You are the Personnel Manager and chairman of the meeting you have called. to take full responsibility for it. You are therefore concerned to find out what everybody thinks, and try to get a consensus of opinion one way or the other. You are very worried about the effect on existing personnel the creation of the post might have.

Paul Malone

You are the Marketing Manager. It is your idea to appoint a product executive, and you should therefore prepare as many arguments as possible in favour of creating the post. You have an assistant to help you.

Dennis Evans

You are the Sales Manager. You are not at all happy about appointing a product executive, as this will take away some of your own responsibilities. You also know that your sales force will resent the Product Executive, and that they are worried they may lose their jobs if more Product Executives are appointed in the future. You should prepare arguments against the proposal.

Charles Spence

You are the Company Secretary. You are very much against Malone's proposal. Five years ago you helped Downes completely reorganize the structure of Bellcrest on extremely economical lines. You are very reluctant to allow the structure to be changed in such a way as to incur extra expense. You do not feel a product executive is at all necessary, and should prepare arguments against it.

Bob Orpenshaw

You are the head of Research and Development. Surprisingly, you are in favour of the idea, not because you are worried about increased sales efficiency, but simply because you want someone to take the paper work on the SC1 out of your hands, thereby giving you more time to concentrate on its actual development. You should prepare arguments in favour of Malone's proposal.

Tom Driver

You are the Production Manager. You are neutral towards Paul Malone's proposal, and are ready to be convinced either way. You are very tired of hearing Charles Spence complaining about the amount of money being spent by the company, and should be prepared to attack him.

James Jackson

You are Malone's assistant. You should therefore assist him in preparing arguments in favour of appointing a product executive.

William Jenkins

You are head of the Overseas Sales Department. You are very much in favour of a product executive, mainly because you have had difficulty in getting satisfactory service facilities for your customers under the present structure of the company. You want to see the Product Executive as a man you can constantly call on to help your overseas customers with visits and advice. You should elaborate arguments to support and extend the scope of Malone's proposals.

Douglas Hamilton

You are Downes' personal assistant. You are acting as an observer in the absence of Downes himself. It is your job to quietly push the idea of a product executive through to a favourable decision without letting anybody know that this is what Downes really wants. You should prepare how you are going to do this. Downes has told you that on no account must you appear to influence the decision of the meeting.

Jean Smith

Your job is to keep the minutes of the meeting and to give a summary of the decisions reached at the end.

EPISODE 5 AWKWARD QUESTIONS

Maurice Downes very much hoped to persuade Ashburnham's Bank not to withdraw the £300,000 loan given to Bellcrest five years before. He did not know who were Bellcrest's rivals for the Bank's money, and so decided to try to arrange a meeting with Sir Frederick Ashburnham to find this out. When his secretary rang up the Bank, Sir Frederick was speaking to someone else and the line was engaged. Downes had to wait until Sir Frederick rang him back.

When Sir Frederick rang Downes back, he enquired if Bellcrest had definite proposals for the Bank to consider. Downes said he would prefer not to go into details, and asked if Sir Frederick could spare twenty minutes to discuss Bellcrest's future. Unfortunately, Sir Frederick was shortly going to Brussels and was then flying on to Switzerland and the United States. Downes was disappointed at being unable to arrange a meeting with Sir Frederick, and was even more disappointed when Sir Frederick suggested he should discuss Bellcrest's future with Edward Needham, who was visiting another of the Bank's customers in Bellcrest's area. Sir Frederick did not tell Downes that the main purpose of Needham's trip to the Midlands was to visit Electrovans.

Downes met Needham for lunch later that day in a second-rate hotel, as Downes had been unable to book his guest into a more suitable one. The meal was very uninteresting, and there was a poor selection of wine. Downes had a tough steal and the meal was made more unpleasant for him by Needham's refusal to drink anything but water.

Downes was also unable to get the information about Bellcrest's rivals for the Bank's money. Throughout the meal Needham was clearly trying not to give anything away, and Downes had to be content with the knowledge that the Bank was comparing Bellcrest's growth rate with that of other companies who were trying to expand and diversify. But Needham failed to draw out Downes on the subject of Bellcrest's plans for diversification.

While Downes was trying to get more information from the Bank, Malone was attempting to get in touch with Urwin before he returned to Canada. Urwin finally rang him up from a petrol station, and agreed to have lunch with him on the following day, Saturday. Malone was slightly worried about entertaining Urwin at home as he had a number of awkward questions to ask him.

The question uppermost in Malone's mind at the time was whether it was Urwin who had offered Orpenshaw a job. This was particularly important to Malone in view of the SC1 to project, but he was unable to get Urwin to talk business until he was just about to leave. When he did manage to bring up the subject, he was surprised to hear that Urwin had offered a job not to Orpenshaw, but to his secretary, who had turned the job down. Urwin added that Malone was not paying enough attention to his secretary.

Just as Urwin was leaving Malone had a telephone call from Bellcrest's security officer, who told him there was a serious fire at the factory.

UNIT SUMMARY

Structures **The structures dealt with in this unit are:**

1 Past Simple contrasted with Past Continuous:
Bellcrest *was running* at a loss even after Downes *took over.*

2 The Future Simple, 'going to', and Present Continuous with future time reference:
The Chairman *will arrive* at 11 a.m.
Downes *is going to visit* Ashburnham this afternoon.
We're starting a market campaign next week.

3 Position of 'Not':
I don't want to discuss this with you immediately.
I'd *prefer not to* discuss that at this point.

Vocabulary **The areas of vocabulary dealt with are:**

1 Ordering a meal in a restaurant.
2 At the petrol station.

dditional Notes

Exercise C

The exercise is contextualized in order to bring out the most appropriate uses in a given context of the three ways of marking future time reference dealt with in this unit. In this exercise it is therefore a question of which form is most *appropriate,* rather than that which is 'grammatically correct'.

Drill 2

This is a cumulative drill, in that the pupil is required to practise the three forms of the future, first in isolation, and then in the final phase to choose which form is most appropriate in the context of the stimulus.

Drills 3 and 4

The teacher is advised to introduce the pupils to the vocabulary used in these drills before going to the language laboratory.

Role Simulation

The teacher should take the part of the waiter and take the orders of the hosts. He should take this opportunity of asking both hosts and guests relevant questions to draw out items of vocabulary from the drills, menus and wine list. He should also take any opportunity that arises to ask questions designed to elicit suitable structures. These questions should be prepared in advance.

The teacher should *not* show pupils the menu and wine list until they are actually seated at the 'dinner-table'. If there are items on the menu or wine list which pupils do not understand, they will be obliged to ask either each other or the 'waiter'/teacher for clarification, which provides useful language practice.

In the interests of realism the teacher should (as far as possible) arrange the classroom to represent a dining-room. If available, a company canteen or other suitable place should be used.

COMPREHENSION QUESTIONS

1 Why did Downes want a meeting with Sir Frederick Ashburnham?
2 Why couldn't Downes speak to Sir Frederick immediately?
3 Did Downes ring again later?
4 What did Sir Frederick ask Downes?
5 Did Downes explain his proposals to Sir Frederick?
6 What reason did Sir Frederick give for not meeting Downes?
7 What did Downes think of this excuse?
8 What did Sir Frederick suggest?
9 Was Downes pleased at the prospect of meeting Needham?
10 What information about Needham did Sir Frederick not give Downes?
11 Where did Downes and Needham have lunch?
12 Why didn't they meet in a better hotel?
13 What sort of a meal did they have?
14 How informative was Needham?
15 What did Needham tell Downes about Bellcrest's growth rate?
16 What was Malone doing while Downes was lunching with Needham?
17 How did Urwin get in touch with Malone?
18 Where did he ring from?
19 Why was Malone worried?
20 What was the most important question on his mind?
21 Why was it so important?
22 Did they talk business all the time?
23 When did they talk business?
24 Who had Urwin offered a job to?
25 How did Malone react to this news?
26 Had his secretary accepted the job?
27 What did Urwin say about Malone's relationship with his secretary?
28 When did the security officer ring Malone?
29 What news did he have?

EXERCISES

Exercise A Complete the following sentences:

1 When people go out they often go to a r. . If they're taking a guest they often b. a t. in advance as in popular restaurants it is sometimes difficult to get a table without a r. . On arrival a w. leads them to a table and brings them a m. . Many restaurants have a w. w. , who brings them the w. l. to show them what there is to drink. It is usual to order the first two c. together, and further c. later in the meal. At the end of the meal a b. will be brought.

2 A car runs on p. . If you're in England you get p. at a p. s. , known in America as a g. s. The a. is the man who serves you. He will usually clean the w. and b. w. for you while you are waiting. If you ask him, he will also t. u. the r. with water, the b. with distilled water, check that your t. are at the right pressure and that you have sufficient o.

Exercise B Make sentences from these notes:

Example:

Bellcrest/run/loss/even after/Downes/takes over.

Bellcrest was running at a loss even after Downes took over.

1 Downes/stop/the SC1 project/when/take over/five years ago.
2 Orpenshaw/work/SC1 project/when/Downes/stop it.
3 Urwin/just/leave/when/Malone/receive/telephone call.
4 Dr Perkins/phone/Malone/while/interview/Beeston.
5 Malone/entertain/Urwin/when/hear/news of fire.
6 Malone/phone/Downes/when/hear/news of fire.
7 When/Downes/ring/Ashburnham/he/find/they/still/consider/withdraw/loan.
8 Hanson/visit/Bellcrest/because/write/series of articles.
9 Malone/dictate/letters/when/Evans/drop in.
10 Urwin/ring/Malone/while/wait/petrol station.

Exercise C *Downes and Malone are discussing the coming visit of the Minister of Science and Technology to the Bellcrest works.*

Complete the sentences with the most appropriate form of the verb, i.e. will do/is going to do/is doing:

Downes: Have you seen this letter from the Ministry?

Malone: Yes. I see they've confirmed the arrangements for the visit.

Downes: Yes. The Minister (come) here next Tuesday. He (arrive) on the 10.30 train.

Malone: Have you any plans for his visit? What (do) he when he gets here?

Downes: Well, we have made one or two plans. We (show) him round the new factory first.

Malone: Right. I (see) that all that stuff left by the builders is cleared up.

Downes: Yes, please do. Oh, and make sure that those electric wires are properly fixed.

Malone: Heavens, yes! I had forgotten about that. Don't worry. I (have) a word with the chief electrician immediately.

Downes: He (talk) to some of the workers on the production line. It's a bit difficult to say how long this (take) possibly about an hour and half. Then we (have) lunch with members of the Board at 12.30. By the way, I haven't done anything about flowers for the table.

Malone: Oh, I have already talked to Jean about that, and she (look after) that.

Downes: Good. Then at two o'clock we (meet) to discuss Government plans to promote exports. They say they (help) companies that want to expand their export markets. If we can convince them that our development projects are sound, they (support) us financially.

Malone: Look. Orpenshaw says he (conduct) tests on the SC1 prototype next week. I'd like the Minister to see that.

Downes: Oh, yes. I promise you we (show) him that.

Malone: When is he due to leave?

Downes: He (travel) to London on the 4.30 train.

Exercise D **Complete the following sentences:**

1 Malone: Doesn't Sam Urwin know about the SC1?
Downes: No, and I (prefer) for the moment.

2 Driver: Are you going to try and persuade Orpenshaw to stay?
Malone: Yes, I (like) at Bellcrest.

3 Malone: Can you finish the report by the end of the week?
Orpenshaw: No, I (expect) until next week.

4 Spence: Can't we give the Bank details of our development project?
Downes: No, I (want) yet.

5 Spence: Why don't you consult Needham? After all, he's on the Board.
Downes: No, I (prefer) about this matter.

6 Orpenshaw: Will you be able to see Urwin before he leaves?
Malone: I'm not sure but I (hope) before he leaves.

7 Malone: What about Williams? He might cause trouble.
Downes: No, I (expect) to cause any trouble.

8 Spence: You'll have to be careful in your dealings with Ashburnham's.
Downes: Yes. I (not like) to withdraw the loan.

9 Downes: Will you get the results of the market survey soon?
Malone: I'm afraid not. I (expect) until the end of the month.

10 Secretary: Do you want to speak to journalists about the fire?
Malone: No, I (prefer) till tomorrow.

Exercise E **Written Task**

Write two letters in answer to this invitation as if you were Maurice Downes, one accepting it and one refusing it.

The Chairman & Board of Directors request the pleasure of your company at a reception to be held to mark the 150th anniversary of the founding of Ashburnham's Merchant Bank on Wednesday, 3rd April, 1972 at 7 p.m.

R.S.V.P. The Secretary to the Board
Ashburnham's Bank,
96 Iberia Street,
London WC29 SH5.

White Tie
Decorations will be worn.

DRILLS

Drill 1 I wonder if my assistant has written the report yet. Could you speak to him?
OH, DON'T WORRY ABOUT THAT. HE WAS WRITING THE REPORT WHEN I SPOKE TO HIM YESTERDAY.

I wonder if the Bank has arranged the loan. Could you ring them up?
OH, DON'T WORRY ABOUT THAT. THEY WERE ARRANGING THE LOAN WHEN I RANG THEM UP YESTERDAY.

Drill 2

a The telephone's ringing but I can't answer it.
DON'T WORRY. I'LL ANSWER IT FOR YOU.

b You could see Ashburnham next week if he wasn't going to Zurich.
OH, OF COURSE, I FORGOT. HE'S GOING TO ZURICH NEXT WEEK.

c Does Jean Smith intend to stay with Bellcrest?
OH, SHE'S CERTAINLY GOING TO STAY WITH BELLCREST.

Dialogue **At the petrol station**

On his way to visit Electrovans, Urwin stops to get some petrol:

Good morning. Six gallons, please.
Super, please. How much is super per gallon, by the way?
The battery's all right, but could you check the oil?
Well, you'd better give me a pint then, please.
Yes, I had the tyres checked only yesterday. Have you got a public telephone here?
Yes, fine. Oh, and would you clean the windscreen while you're at it?

Drill 3 *You are the host for dinner at a restaurant. The waiter has brought the menu, and you must offer various dishes to your guests.*

Waiter: Would you like any soup, sir?
NOW WHAT WOULD YOU LIKE? THERE'S ASPARAGUS, OR TOMATO OR PERHAPS YOU'D PREFER FRENCH ONION.

SOUP
Asparagus, tomato, French onion

FISH
Haddock, turbot, sole

MAIN COURSE
Roast beef, lamb chops, omelette

VEGETABLES
Spinach, broccoli, peas
Potatoes: boiled, roast, French fried

SWEETS
Fruit salad, trifle, ice-cream

COFFEE
English, Irish, Turkish

WINES
Claret, burgundy, hock

LIQUEURS
Cointreau, Crême de Menthe, Brandy.

Drill 4 *You are the guest at dinner. Unfortunately, you don't eat fish, and you don't drink beer.*

Now what would you like? The sole is very good here.
WELL, IF YOU DON'T MIND, I'D PREFER NOT TO HAVE FISH.

Well, what about an omelette?
THAT SOUNDS VERY NICE. YES, I'LL HAVE AN OMELETTE, PLEASE.

ACTIVE LISTENING

Paul Malone has invited Sam Urwin to lunch. He and Janet are planning the meal.

1 Where does their conversation take place?

....

....

2 Why didn't Paul tell Janet earlier?

....

....

3 Why is Saturday a bad day for Janet?

....

....

4 What is her attitude to Urwin?

....

5 What is the main thing they must decide?

. . . .

. . . .

6 Why doesn't Janet want to have steak?

. . . .

. . . .

7 What does she choose for the first course and why?

. . . .

. . . .

8 Why do they decide not to have a sweet?

. . . .

. . . .

9 Have they already got the wine?

. . . .

. . . .

10 Why does Paul suggest going out the following Wednesday, and where will they go?

. . . .

. . . .

ROLE SIMULATION

Statement of Problem

Maurice Downes has three guests for dinner, Paul Malone and Dennis Evans each have two. None of the guests are English native speakers. For the sake of convenience, they have decided to entertain their seven guests together, and have booked a table for ten at the Crouch End Hotel, Leicester.

After a pleasant drink in the bar, they have led their guests into the dining-room and the waiter has presented the menu and the wine list.

The hosts now have to order the various courses for their guests, and explain the menu where necessary. They then have to entertain the guests for half an hour.

Written follow-up

Downes, Malone and Evans should write a letter to one of their guests thanking them for their visit.

The guests should write a letter thanking their hosts for their hospitality.

DESCRIPTION OF ROLES

Maurice Downes

Your three guests are from a South-East Asian company who wish to become your sole agents for electronic components in this area. You have spent the day discussing this with them.

)ownes' Guests

a You have come to Bellcrest to try to get your company appointed as sole agents for Bellcrest's products in South-East Asia. For religious reasons you don't eat fish. You find European food inferior and prefer spiced dishes. Choose your own name.

b You have come to Bellcrest to try to get your company appointed as sole agents for Bellcrest's products in South-East Asia. You have a stomach ulcer. Choose Your own name.

c You have come to Bellcrest to try to get your company appointed as sole agents for Bellcrest's products in South-East Asia. You believe all alcoholic drinks to be immoral. Choose your own name.

Paul Malone

Your two guests are potential customers, whom you are anxious to impress.

ʌlalone's Guests

a You are thoroughly enjoying your visit and are looking forward to a good meal. You prefer German wines to French wines. You represent a company that is interested in buying electronic components from Bellcrest. Choose your own name.

b You are suffering from a mild stomach disorder, and cannot bear the smell of melon. You want mineral water to drink, and light food. You represent a company that is interested in buying electronic equipment from Bellcrest. Choose your own name.

Dennis Evans

Your two guests are two of your most important customers. Your purpose is to promote friendly relations between the two companies.

:vans' Guests

a Your company buys regularly from Bellcrest. You are a vegetarian, and adore Portuguese wines. You hate the smell of fish. Unfortunately, you're driving and can't drink.

b Your company buys regularly from Bellcrest. You have no particular likes or dislikes as far as food is concerned, but you are very particular about the wine you drink.

TABLE D'HÔTE DINNER

3 courses – £1.05

* * *

Fruit Juice
Chilled Honeydew Melon
OYSTERS – Wivenhoe Natives – £1.00 ½ doz.
Cream of Chicken
Shrimp Cocktail

* * *

Fillets of Plaice Meunière
Roast Beef and Yorkshire Pudding
Roast Best Ends of Lamb with
Mint Sauce or Redcurrant Jelly
Braised Ribs of Scotch Beef Jardinière

* * *

Omelettes   Cold Buffet
Fresh Lobster Dishes Cooked to Order
– 65p.
Bouquetière of vegetables

* * *

Sweets to Choice from the Trolley
Cheese and Biscuits
Fresh Cream – 10p.
Coffee – 10p.

Service not included.

WINE LIST

		Bottle	½ Bottle
Red Burgundy			
Beaujolais Villages 1969		1.20	0.60
Macon Rouge 1969		0.85	0.43
Vintage 1959			
*Chambertin		1.45	0.75
*Gevrey-Chambertin		1.75	0.90
Vintage 1964			
Volnay		1.20	0.60
*Pommard		1.30	0.65
White Burgundy			
Meursault 1967		1.20	0.60
*Chablis 1967		1.20	0.60
Claret			
St. Emilion les Fleurs NV		0.90	0.45
Vintage 1960			
+Château Lafitte		3.00	1.50
+Château Lyenné		1.30	0.65
+Chateau Malplaquet		2.25	1.15
White Bordeaux			
Medium Dry	Entre deux Mers NV	0.80	0.40
	Chateau Didier NV	0.85	0.43
Medium Sweet	Leveau NV	0.70	0.35
Sweet	Sauternes Blanche NV	0.90	0.45
	Barsac NV	0.90	0.45
Hock			
Liebfraumilch Rhinemaiden		1.12½	0.57
‡Liebfraumilch Blue Nun		1.25	0.62½
Johannisberger Riesling		0.92½	0.47
Niersteiner Rheinberg		0.70	0.35
Moselle			
Berncasteler Yellow label 1968		1.10	0.55
‡Schloss Ürzig-Spätlese 1969		1.30	0.65
‡Cochemer Sonnenuhr-Auslese 1969		1.80	0.90
Other Wines			
Rosé d'Anjou		0.76	0.38
Le Rhône Rosé		0.80	0.40
Gewürztraminer		1.35	0.68
Asti Spumanti		1.30	0.65

\+ Chateau bottled

* Bottled in France

‡ Bottled in Germany

EPISODE 6 THE FIRE

As soon as Malone heard about the fire, he telephoned Downes, who was having lunch with Needham at the time. Malone, Downes and Needham all hurried immediately to the factory. The fire had started in an old warehouse, which had already been destroyed. Now the fire brigade were trying to prevent the fire from spreading. To do this they had to soak the research and development area, and the water was going to cause a lot of damage.

Needham was particularly concerned about whether the buildings had been insured, but Downes was able to reassure him on this point. The warehouse building was insured for £50,000 and the policy also covered the finished goods held in stock in the warehouse. He reminded Needham that it had been he who had questioned the premium Bellcrest paid, and so he should have known this.

They were interrupted by a journalist, Joy Banks. Downes admitted that if the fire spread it would be a disaster for Bellcrest. Joy Banks used his words out of context, and on Monday morning the Midland News headline quoted Downes as saying that the fire had been a disaster for the company.

This unfortunate publicity was bound to have a bad effect on Bellcrest shares, as Needham was quick to point out the following day. He offered to get the Bank's Public Relations agents to handle the press, radio and television, and Downes gratefully accepted.

The fire brought problems to everyone at Bellcrest. Most of Bellcrest's finished goods had been destroyed, quite apart from the damage done to the research and development area. Tom Driver, the Production Manager, had to deal with the most urgent problems. Production would have to be increased to make up for the losses, and he had to find additional storage space for new stocks. He also had to meet the insurance adjuster.

Spence, the Company Secretary, was concerned about the financial position of the company. Bellcrest had lost £200,000 worth of stocks, and he had to put in a claim to the insurance company as soon as possible. Evans naturally had dozens of telephone calls from customers worried about delays to their deliveries. Orpenshaw's research and development area had been soaked to prevent the fire from spreading. Water was nearly as bad as fire, and there had been a lot of damage. This meant that work on the SC1 might be held up.

While he was tidying up the mess, Needham came in and in his disappointment Orpenshaw unintentionally revealed the existence of a new development project, although he didn't mention the SC1 by name. This had been something Downes had particularly wanted to avoid, as he hadn't wanted the Bank to know anything about the SC1 until the Board had approved the project.

At twelve o'clock Downes held a management meeting to discuss the problems created by the fire. He invited Needham to attend. Driver was the first to describe his problems in detail. Additional storage space had to be found for finished goods, but if he re-allocated parts of the factory for storage purposes, production would be bound to suffer. Downes concluded that they might be obliged to look outside Bellcrest for the extra storage space they needed. Driver added that the factory would have to work to capacity for several weeks, and that overtime would almost certainly be needed as well.

Spence then went into the financial consequences of the fire. He said that Bellcrest were bound to have a short-term liquidity problem, and gave four reasons for this: the insurance claim would not be met for some time, Bellcrest would not be able to invoice customers for several weeks and at the same time would have to meet extra wage bills and the cost of renting new storage space.

At this point Needham was called away by an urgent phone call, and Malone immediately brought up the subject of the effect of the fire on the development of the SC1. Downes, however, refused to discuss it. He pointed out that the immediate need was to satisfy Bellcrest's customers. Malone replied that the obvious solution was to concentrate on the product lines that brought in the quickest returns and the largest profits, but went on to add that he did not think this was the course Bellcrest should follow. He recommended that Bellcrest should look after regular customers as far as possible, but pay special attention to overseas customers, who would be likely to bring in Bellcrest's long-term profits. The loss of overseas customers at this time would have a serious effect on the company's long-term growth. Evans had arranged to visit the more important U.K. customers, and it was agreed that Malone should visit customers and agents in Europe.

As the meeting broke up, Downes pointed out to Malone that unless the immediate problems were solved there would be no development of the SC1.

UNIT SUMMARY

Structures **The structures dealt with in this unit are:**

1 Ways of expressing obligation:

We *must* meet our commitments.
We *had to* abandon the project.
We *shall have to* reconsider our position.
We *were obliged to* withdraw from negotiations.

2 Past Simple contrasted with Present Perfect:

Malone *visited* overseas customers *last year.*
Evans *has just returned* from London.

3 Future Continuous:

I *shall be attending* a meeting on Friday morning.

Vocabulary **The areas of vocabulary dealt with in this unit are:**

1 Insurance
2 Liquidity/cash flow

Additional Notes

Exercise D

This is a two phase oral exercise. In the first phase the teacher should take the part of the questioner, (a) in the examples, choosing only those times which are given in the diary. The pupil consults his diary and gives the appropriate answer, (b) in the examples.

In the second phase, the pupils are required to ask the questions. If desired, the pupils may ask questions outside the scope of the diary.

Dialogue

The 'shadowing' of a role is omitted from this and subsequent dialogues in the course. From this point on the teacher should insist that his pupils practise the utterances thoroughly enough to enable them to take their part in the dialogue with their books shut.

COMPREHENSION QUESTIONS

1 What was the first thing Malone did when he heard about the fire?
2 Where was Downes?
3 Where had the fire started?
4 Had the warehouse been saved?
5 What were the fire brigade trying to do?
6 What did they have to do in order to succeed?
7 What effect would this have?
8 What was Needham worried about?
9 Was the warehouse insured?
10 Were the stocks covered by the policy?
11 Who had questioned the premium?
12 Who interrupted Downes and Needham?
13 What did Downes tell her?
14 Did Joy Banks report his words accurately?
15 What did the Midland News say on Monday morning?
16 What effect would the bad publicity have?
17 What did Needham offer Downes?
18 Were all Bellcrest's finished goods destroyed?
19 What other damage had been done?

20 Who had the most urgent problems?
21 What were his problems?
22 What worried Spence?
23 How much had Bellcrest lost?
24 What did he have to do?
25 Who telephoned Evans?
26 Why did they telephone him?
27 What effect had water had on Orpenshaw's research and development area?
28 What did this mean for Orpenshaw?
29 Who interrupted Orpenshaw?
30 Did Orpenshaw mean to tell Needham about development projects?
31 Did he tell Needham about the SC1?
32 Why didn't Downes want the Bank to know about the SC1?
33 When was the management meeting?
34 Why was it called?
35 What did Driver have to find?
36 What was bound to suffer if he used the factory to store goods in?
37 What was Downes' reaction to Driver's problem?
38 What other problems did Driver have?
39 What did Spence talk about?
40 What were Bellcrest bound to have?
41 What is a short-term liquidity problem?
42 Why would Bellcrest have a short-term liquidity problem?
43 Why did Needham leave the meeting?
44 What subject did Malone bring up?
45 What did Downes see as a more urgent problem than the SC1?
46 What was the obvious answer?
47 Did Malone recommend this solution?
48 What did Malone recommend?
49 Why did he recommend this?
50 What was Evans going to do?
51 Where was Malone going?

EXERCISES

Exercise A **Complete the following sentences:**

1 Needham was very concerned about whether the warehouse destroyed in the fire had been i. . Downes told him that the building had been i. f. £50,000, and that the p. also c. the stocks in the building. He told Needham that Bellcrest paid the i. c. a high p. . The following day the i. a. came to discuss Bellcrest's c. for the damage caused by the fire.

2 Spence told the meeting that Bellcrest would be short of cash for several weeks. He gave a number of reasons for this s. t. l. problem. Firstly, Bellcrest would not get c. from the insurance company immediately, as it would take time for the i. u. to meet the claim. Secondly, the company would not be able to i. customers, as there would be no goods being delivered. At the same time, he had to secure a short-term c. f. to meet extra wage bills for overtime.

Exercise B 1 *It is the Monday morning after the fire at Bellcrest.*

Make sentences from these notes, saying what people had to do at the time of the fire, and will have to do as a result of the fire.

Examples:
Security Officer/telephone/fire brigade.
The Security Officer had to telephone the fire brigade.

Needham/meet/Public Relations agents/this afternoon.
Needham will have to meet the Public Relations agents this afternoon.

a Fire brigade/prevent/fire/spread.
b Driver/find/additional storage space.
c Firemen/soak/R and D area.
d Malone/phone/Downes/immediately.
e Spence/put in/claim/insurance company.
f Miss Banks/interview/Downes.
g Malone/visit/customers in Europe.
h Press/take/photographs of the fire.
i Orpenshaw/tidy up/mess/soon as/can.
j Downes/stay up/most of the night.

2 *Downes and Needham are discussing what is bound to happen after the fire, and what they are obliged to do about it.*

Complete the sentences using 'bound to/obliged to'.

Downes: I'm afraid the damage is very serious. Production be affected and we be very short of storage space.

Needham: Do you mean you'll find storage space outside the factory?

Downes: Yes, I think we'll have to. And all the staff will ______ work overtime until we're on our feet again. Also the fire ______ delay the research work considerably.

Needham: Yes, I was just talking to Orpenshaw who has ______ tidy up the mess over there.

Exercise C *Mr Barker of Beamish Motors is writing to Malone about Alan Beeston.*

Complete the letter, choosing the appropriate verb form:

BEAMISH MOTORS LTD

23 Elder Road,
Birmingham 13.

PRIVATE AND CONFIDENTIAL
Our ref: PB/0095

Telephone: 021-839 2532

12th July, 1971.

P. Malone, Esq.,
Bellcrest Ltd.,
Leicester.

Dear Mr. Malone,

Alan Beeston

Thank you for your letter of 8th July, 1971.

Mr. Beeston (come) ______ to us last October on a year's contract. During his time here he (show) ______ considerable ability in his work and (be) ______ a useful member of our team. He (take) ______ a degree in electronic engineering at Manchester University eight years ago and (join) ______ the Ministry of Defence when he (leave) ______ university. His experience in negotiating contracts for the Ministry (be) ______ very valuable in his work here.

I (know) ______ Mr Beeston for five years and my experience of him leads me to believe that the work he (do) ______ at the Ministry after leaving University and the excellent work he (already do) ______ for us make him first class material for a post such as technical salesman or product executive.

Yours sincerely,

Peter Barker
Personnel Manager.

Exercise D *Example:*

a *Can I see you at 10 on Monday, the 6th?*

b *I'm afraid not. I'll be talking to journalists at 10, but I'll be free in the afternoon.*

DIARY

Monday
6th Talk to journalists 10 a.m.

Tuesday
7th Revise delivery dates with Evans 2.45

Wednesday
8th Speak to sales force 9.15

Thursday
9th Call on M.P. Consultants 10.30 a.m.

Friday
10th Discuss new designs with Orpenshaw 9.15

DIARY

Monday
13th Review the development projects with Downes 10.15

Tuesday
14th Meet Davidson's agent 9.45

Wednesday
15th Show visitors round new plant 2.30

Thursday
16th Attend Committee 11.00
Lunch with Spence 1.00

Friday
17th Interview candidates for post of Assistant Site Engineer 3.00

Exercise E **Written Task**

You are the chief buyer for a firm that deals with Bellcrest. You have learnt about the fire at their factory. Write a letter to Bellcrest. Use these notes.

just seen headlines
placed an order for . . . . early last month
require urgently . . . . not yet arrived
unfortunately if Bellcrest cannot supply . . . .

DRILLS

Drill 1 *The management at Bellcrest are discussing what to do after the fire.*

Should we ask the Bank for more money?
NO, I DON'T THINK SO. BUT I DO THINK WE SHOULD ASK FOR MORE TIME TO REPAY THE LOAN.

Are we obliged to meet existing delivery dates?
NO, I DON'T THINK SO. BUT I DO THINK WE'RE OBLIGED TO EXPLAIN THE POSITION TO OUR CUSTOMERS.

1 Ask/more time/repay/loan
2 Explain/position/our customers
3 Make/statement
4 Look/security arrangements
5 Work out/cost/damage
6 Remember/importance/long-term profits
7 Consider/short-term liquidity problem
8 Review/all our projects
9 Consider priorities/this area
10 Find/extra storage space/finished goods

Drill 2 We'll be in trouble if they withdraw the loan.
FORTUNATELY FOR US THEY HAVEN'T WITHDRAWN THE LOAN YET.

Of course we won't be able to invoice our customers for some time.
FORTUNATELY FOR US WE INVOICED OUR CUSTOMERS LAST WEDNESDAY.

1 Not yet
2 Last Wednesday
3 Last week
4 A few days ago
5 Just
6 Always – so far
7 Already
8 Last December
9 Never before
10 Yesterday

Dialogue **Talking to the Press**

Maurice Downes is interrupted by the journalist, Joy Banks, who has a number of questions to ask him.

Yes?
I can't give you a definite answer at the moment.
Yes, our insurance naturally covers everything.
Compensation?
Excuse me, I've forgotten your name.
Well, Miss Banks, I don't think this is the time to be talking about compensation. Now, if you'll excuse me, we're all very busy.
A press statement will be issued tomorrow morning. I have no further comment at this stage, Miss Banks.

Drill 3 *The Management Committee is meeting to discuss action after the fire. Downes, the Chairman, wants to make clear the priorities in the discussion.*

Don't you think it would be a good idea to talk to the Press?
OUR MAIN CONCERN NOW IS RESTARTING PRODUCTION, NOT TALKING TO THE PRESS.

1 Restart production
2 Find storage space
3 Build up stocks
4 Reassure customers
5 Service urgent orders
6 Solve the immediate problems
7 Bring in some money
8 Get quick returns

Drill 4 *Now the Committee is taking quick decisions. Downes does not ask for a formal vote, but simply asks if everyone is agreed.*

I feel we should make a statement to the Press.
CAN I TAKE IT WE'RE AGREED ON MAKING A STATEMENT TO THE PRESS?

Now Downes goes a step further, and suggests the action which is required.

I feel we should make a statement to the Press.
CAN I TAKE IT WE'RE AGREED ON MAKING A STATEMENT TO THE PRESS, IN WHICH CASE I'LL PREPARE A DRAFT.

1 Prepare draft
2 Tom Driver/make arrangements
3 Personnel Manager/issue notice
4 Paul/discuss it with Dennis Evans
5 Charles Spence/prepare statement
6 Paul/give instructions/Orpenshaw
7 Tom Driver/put up proposal
8 Miss Armstrong/circulate agenda

ACTIVE LISTENING

Mr Barrington, the insurance adjuster, visits Bellcrest after the fire. He is questioning Tom Driver about the fire.

1 Why wasn't the fire discovered immediately?

. . . .

. . . .

2 What had happened by the time the fire was discovered?

. . . .

. . . .

3 What action did the watchman take?

. . . .

. . . .

4 How badly damaged was the warehouse?

. . . .

. . . .

5 What was kept there?

. . . .

. . . .

6 What other damage had been done and what had caused it?

. . . .

. . . .

7 Does Driver know the value of this?

. . . .

. . . .

8 What new safety measures were Bellcrest considering at the time?

. . . .

. . . .

9 Who has all the information about Bellcrest's insurance policy?

. . . .

. . . .

10 Was the warehouse old-fashioned?

. . . .

. . . .

11 What is Bellcrest's system for keeping records?

. . . .

. . . .

12 Why were the stock records not lost in the fire?

. . . .

. . . .

ROLE SIMULATION

Statement of Problem

Maurice Downes has called a management meeting to hear reports from managers and heads of departments on the damage caused by the fire and to discuss what action should be taken to minimize its effects on the fortunes of Bellcrest.

You should re-enact this meeting and come to your own decision as to what action should be taken. Those present at the meeting will be Maurice Downes, in the chair, Paul Malone, Dennis Evans, Edward Needham, Tom Driver, Bob Orpenshaw, Charles Spence, David Smithson (Personnel Manager), Douglas Hamilton (Downes' assistant) and Miss Armstrong (Downes' secretary).

Ground plan of Bellcrest Ltd.

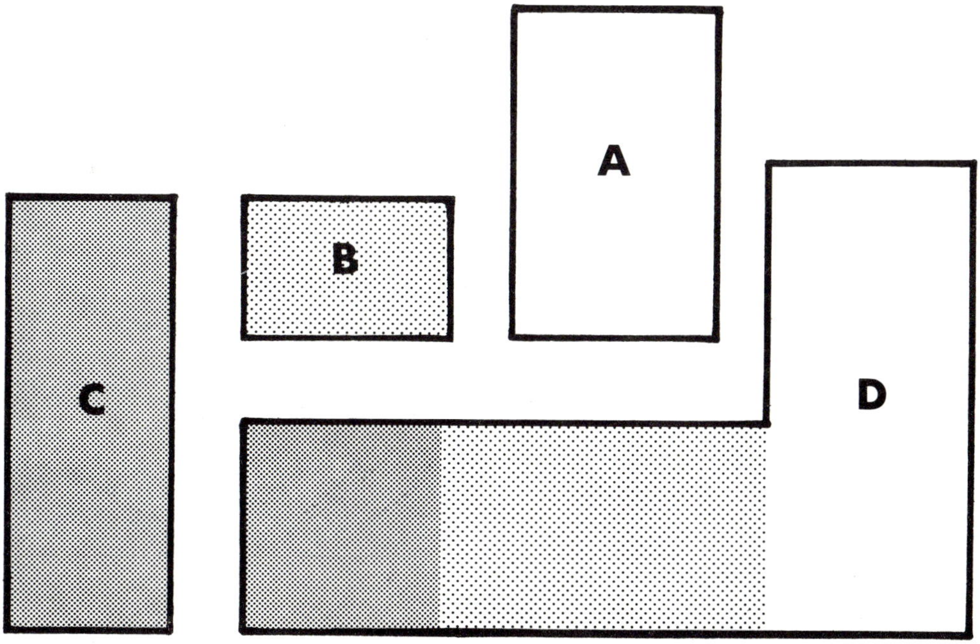

A Headquarters (Administrative/Personnel/Sales/Finance Departments)
B Research and Development Area
C Warehouse
D Factory

Destroyed by the fire.

Soaked in water by the fire brigade.

Written follow-up Write a report to a subsidiary company in Europe describing the effect of the fire and what action Bellcrest is going to take as decided at your meeting.

DESCRIPTION OF ROLES

Maurice Downes

You have been up all night and are in a very bad temper. You want accurate reports from your subordinates with concrete and realistic proposals as to how problems can be overcome. You should prepare an agenda for yourself listing the points that you wish to raise and the order in which you wish to raise them.

Paul Malone

You are aware of the fact that, with £200,000 worth of finished goods destroyed and some damage to the factory itself, you are not going to be able to deliver many of your customers' orders to schedule. However, you are far more concerned with the damage to the research and development area and its effect on the SC1, and really only want to discuss this. You should therefore prepare a short report on the effects the fire will have on deliveries to overseas customers (which you should invent) and then attempt to draw the discussion on to development projects. At the same time you must not let Needham know about the SC1.

Dennis Evans

You should prepare a short report on how the fire will affect deliveries to U.K. customers. Remember that most of your finished goods have been destroyed. You want your U.K. customers to have priority over overseas customers on available stocks and on goods as they are manufactured. You want to abandon overseas customers for the time being.

Edward Needham

Remember that you represent the Bank, not Bellcrest. You should be prepared to state what action the Bank's Public Relations agents have taken to deal with the Press, radio and television. Beyond that, your main concern at the meeting is not to solve the problems, but to find out what development projects Bellcrest are working on.

Tom Driver

You have the most difficult problem. Your warehouse has been destroyed and there is no factory space available for storage purposes. Part of your factory has been burnt out, part soaked in water. You should prepare a short report on the extent of the damage (which you may make as terrible as you like). You should also be ready to state what problems in production there will be over the next few weeks, what your production capacity will be and what extra money you will need from Charles Spence.

Bob Orpenshaw

You are in despair. Your area has been soaked in water, which has destroyed a lot of your equipment and nearly all your documents. You haven't bothered to prepare a proper report, as in your opinion it will be months before the SC1 project can start up again, or any other project for that matter, and you don't care who knows it.

Charles Spence
You should prepare a short report on the financial problems faced by the company as a result of the fire. You cannot naturally make a detailed assessment of the situation until you hear all the details from your colleagues. You should therefore press them to tell you exactly what damage has been done, what will have to be replaced and what extra resources they will need, so that you may work out your assessment in more detail. You should also be in a position to state what action will have to be taken by you to meet the company's financial problems.

David Smithson
You are the Personnel Manager. You should draw up a short report on the effect the fire has had on employees and the consequences. A lot of the work force has had to be laid off due to damage to the factory, and there is great concern about possible loss of jobs. You also want to know whether extra labour will be required, how much and whether skilled or unskilled, to meet the present crisis. There is also the question of overtime.

Douglas Hamilton
You are Downes' assistant. You have been making your own enquiries as to the effect the fire has had. You should prepare a brief report on the results of your enquiries (invent this). You are very concerned to get quick decisions out of everybody present.

Miss Armstrong
You should take the minutes of the meeting and give a summary of decisions reached at the end. Don't let Downes forget anything.

THE MARKET PLACE

Malone had to break off his work on the SC1 as it was necessary for him to visit important customers on the continent. He gave Jean his instructions as to his travel arrangements and went on to mention that Urwin had told him about his offering her a job. Jean replied that she had turned the job down, but on Malone's asking her why she had rejected the offer, she merely said that she had her reasons.

At this point Dennis Evans interrupted them. In view of inevitable delayed delivery dates, it was essential to get in touch with all Bellcrest's customers. Malone and Evans agreed that the sales force should approach customers individually and follow this up with something in writing. Malone emphasized that customers should be reassured that Bellcrest could still deliver the goods, and added that Evans himself should visit as many customers as possible after sending out an explanatory letter. Evans was not happy about writing this letter. as he felt he was better at talking than at writing, but Malone refused to write it for him, although he pointed out that it should go out over the Managing Director's signature. Evans found this letter extremely difficult to write.

Later that week, Evans and one of his salesmen, Finch, set out to visit Western Telecommunications. Finch was confident that Dobson, Western Telecommunications' chief buyer, would be easy to handle, but when Evans saw that Dobson was expecting a large order of surge diverters by the end of the month, he wasn't so sure. On meeting Dobson, Evans didn't waste time making excuses or explaining Bellcrest's problems, but came straight to the point and asked whether Western Telecommunications had sufficient stocks to enable Bellcrest to re-schedule its deliveries. By checking the stock levels, Finch established that Western Telecommunications had enough surge diverters to last for several months and that it would therefore be possible to re-schedule deliveries without disrupting Western Telecommunications' production.

In spite of this, Dobson indicated that he was concerned about being over-dependent on Bellcrest for supplies, and pointed out that he would have found it almost impossible to find alternative supplies at short notice if the fire at Bellcrest had been bad enough to halt production for several months. He said that he had had several attractive offers from some of Bellcrest's competitors, although he hoped it wouldn't be necessary to turn to any of them. On signing the visitors' book on their way out. Evans found that a representative of an Electrovans subsidiary had already called on Western Telecommunications.

While Evans continued his tour of customers, Malone was preparing to set off for the Continent. Before he left, Bob Orpenshaw told him there was something he ought to know. He told Malone that he had decided to turn down the job he had been offered and went on to add that it was Donald Williams who had approached him. This didn't surprise Malone. Orpenshaw then revealed that Electrovans was working on an AC speed control device similar to the one patented by Bellcrest, and drew the conclusion that, as Electrovans' prototype infringed the Bellcrest patents, Williams wanted him to alter the design just enough to enable Electrovans to take out its own patent. Malone was naturally angry, and said that he would make sure that Williams learned about patents and their protection by law.

On arriving at the air terminal, Malone unexpectedly ran into Donald Williams returning from abroad.

UNIT SUMMARY

Structures The structures dealt with in this unit are:

1 He *told* her *to make* the travel arrangements.
contrasted with
He *told* her *he would make* the travel arrangements.

2 Gerund versus Infinitive:

a Verbs followed by an infinitive contrasted with those followed by a Gerund:
Do you *want to attend* the meeting?
Do you *mind attending* the meeting?

b Verb + Preposition + Gerund:
I am *interested in buying* your equipment.

3 Adjective + Infinitive:

It is { important / essential / not enough } to revise the sales forecasts.

It is left to the teacher to work out his own oral introduction to these structures.

Vocabulary The areas of vocabulary dealt with in this unit are:

1 Sales (salesman, sales manager etc)
2 Deliveries/stocks
3 Patents

dditional Notes Exercise D

This is a two phase exercise. In the first phase the pupils are invited to make single sentences, e.g.
'It is important to diversify our product range.'
In the second phase the pupil's statement is countered by an objection from a second pupil, e.g.
'It is important to diversify our product range' – first pupil.
'Yes, but it's more important to keep down costs' – second pupil.

COMPREHENSION QUESTIONS

1 Why did Malone have to stop working on the SC1?
2 What instructions did he give Jean?
3 What did he go on to say?
4 What did Jean answer?
5 Had Jean accepted the offer?
6 What reason did Jean give for rejecting the offer?
7 Why was it essential to get in touch with Bellcrest's customers?
8 How did Malone and Evans think the sales force should approach customers?
9 How did they agree this should be followed up?
10 What point did Malone think should be emphasized to customers?
11 What did he feel Evans should do?
12 When should Evans visit clients?

13 What sort of letter should Evans write?
14 Why did Evans not want to write the explanatory letter?
15 Did Malone offer to write the letter for him?
16 Who should sign the letter?
17 When did Evans visit Western Telecommunications?
18 Who went with Evans?
19 Did Finch think he could handle Dobson?
20 Did Evans agree with Finch?
21 Why didn't Evans agree with Finch?
22 Did Evans explain Bellcrest's problems to Dobson?
23 What did Evans ask Dobson?
24 How did Finch find out that Western Telecommunications had large stocks?
25 How long would stocks last?
26 What did this mean?
27 What was Dobson worried about?
28 Why was he concerned about being over-dependent on Bellcrest for supplies?
29 What kind of offers had Dobson had?
30 Which company had already sent a representative to Western Telecommunications?
31 When did Evans find this out?
32 When did Orpenshaw visit Malone?
33 What had Orpenshaw decided?
34 Who had offered Orpenshaw a job?
35 What device did Orpenshaw say Electrovans was working on?
36 Why did Williams want Orpenshaw to alter Electrovans' design?
37 By how much did Williams want Orpenshaw to alter the design?
38 What did Malone say he would tell Williams?
39 When did Malone meet Williams?
40 Did Malone expect to meet Williams at the terminal?
41 Where was Williams coming back from?

EXERCISES

Exercise A **Complete the following sentences:**

1 Most companies employ a number of to sell their products. Collectively they are known as the and they come under the direction of the Occasionally it is necessary for a company to launch a , also known as a , in order to promote sales of a particular product. In such a campaign the salesmen look for new for the product, which means finding new customers.

2 Western Telecommunications buy their components from Bellcrest, and they do this according to a s. in order to ensure regular d. . On arrival the components are added to existing s. held by the. company. Information concerning components delivered and issued from stock is fed into a computer, which maintains s. c. and can give accurate information on s. l. at any time. Before they bought the computer Dobson's head storeman had to count the components himself every month, which made s. -t. an extremely tiresome job.

3 When a new invention is made, the inventor usually a. for a p. to stop other people from copying his design. Once it has been t. o. the law protects the patent from being i. by others.

Exercise B **Make sentences from these notes:**

1 Malone/tell/Jean/get/travel documents.
2 Malone/tell/Jean/make/travel arrangements/himself.
3 Downes/tell/Miss Armstrong/book/his own/hotel room.
4 Orpenshaw/tell/Malone/refuse/job.
5 Malone/tell/his secretary/take a letter.
6 Driver/tell/Downes/need extra storage space.
7 Spence/tell/Downes/be/short-term liquidity problem.
8 Malone/tell/Jean/arrange/his own/flights.
9 Malone/tell/Jean/arrange/flights.
10 Downes/tell/Miss Armstrong/telephone/Sir Frederick.

Exercise C **Complete these sentences:**

1 I look forward (hear) from you.
2 We couldn't prevent them (turn to) Electrovans.
3 Would you mind (wait) a moment?
4 We are interested (buy) 500 of your Model YZ camera.
5 I don't see the point (discuss) this question at this stage.
6 These measures will enable us (increase) production.
7 We are relying (receive) the goods by the end of the week.
8 I haven't finished (draw up) my proposals yet.
9 Did you remember (bring) that report, Miss Smith?
10 You don't seem (understand) what I'm saying.
11 He suggested (re-schedule) our deliveries.
12 He insists (see) you personally, sir.

Exercise D **Make sentences from the table below:**

Example:

a) It is important to diversify our product range.

b) Yes, but it's <u>more</u> important to keep down costs.

It	is	(more)	important	to diversify	our product range
The fire	was	(not)	essential	to halt	costs
			difficult	to increase	our position
			bad enough	to keep down	production
			serious enough	to strengthen	our sales
				to slow up	

Exercise E **Written task**

Write Dennis Evans' letter to customers setting out the consequences of the fire at Bellcrest. Use these notes:

Fire at factory

Destroyed nearly all finished goods

Delayed delivery dates

Salesman will visit/review stock position

Reassure customer of Bellcrest's ability to deliver the goods ordered

DRILLS

Drill 1 *Paul Malone is giving his secretary instructions about his journey to the Continent.*

1 Make the travel arrangements, Jean.
HE TOLD HER TO MAKE THE TRAVEL ARRANGEMENTS.

2 I'll pick up the tickets myself, Jean.
HE TOLD HER HE WOULD PICK UP THE TICKETS HIMSELF.

Drill 2 *When he returns from his tour of customers, Dennis Evans reports to Downes.*

1 Will they receive the goods on time? They're concerned about that.
I SEE. THEY'RE CONCERNED ABOUT RECEIVING THE GOODS ON TIME.

2 Their supplies mustn't be re-scheduled. They don't want that.
I SEE. THEY DON'T WANT THEIR SUPPLIES TO BE RE-SCHEDULED.

Dialogue **Making Reservations**

On one of his visits to England, Sam Urwin telephones a travel agent.

Yes, can you tell me the times of flights to Munich on the evening of the 15th, please?
Could you book me on the 5.45 flight?
No, first class, please.
Single, please.
Urwin. U-R-W-I-N.
Grand Hotel, Cononation Avenue, W.1.
There's one more thing. When should I check in?
Thank you very much. Goodbye.

Drill 3 *Dennis Evans and the Sales Representatives are discussing the effects of the fire on their customers' orders for the RN1 components.*

1 Look, Dennis, if we're going to satisfy everybody, it's obvious that we must increase production of the RN1.
THAT'S JUST THE POINT. THE FACT IS WE CAN'T INCREASE PRODUCTION OF THE RN1.

2 Well, if we cut production of the other products we could do it.
THAT'S JUST THE POINT. THE FACT IS WE CAN'T CUT PRODUCTION OF THE OTHER PRODUCTS.

Drill 4 *Tom Driver and Dennis Evans are discussing their problems after the Bellcrest fire. Evans has some ideas.*

Our immediate problem is simply to meet the orders on hand.
IT SEEMS TO ME THAT THERE ARE TWO WAYS OF MEETING THE ORDERS ON HAND.

Now listen to Evans when he makes suggestions about how to solve the problems.

Our immediate problem is simply to meet the orders on hand.
IT SEEMS TO ME THAT THERE ARE TWO WAYS OF MEETING THE ORDERS ON HAND. FIRST, BY INCREASING PRODUCTION, AND SECOND, BY RESCHEDULING DELIVERIES.

1 increase production/reschedule deliveries
2 delay some orders/reduce others
3 work overtime/take on new staff
4 explain position/guarantee new delivery dates
5 replan transport/check stock levels
6 write to them/visit them
7 review all orders on hand/consult salesmen
8 use factory space/rent other buildings

ACTIVE LISTENING

George and Harry are two executives of Western Telecommunications, one of Bellcrest's customers. They are discussing how the fire will affect their orders.

1 What reassurance has Evans given them in his letter?

....

....

2 What does Evans fail to mention in the letter?

....

....

3 Why is Western Telecommunications in a difficult position?

....

....

4 What does George want to know in order to judge the extent of their problem?

....

....

5 What is the position as regards RN2's?

....

....

6 Why is this?

....

....

7 What did Harry do as soon as he got the letter?

....

....

8 What does George think the purpose of Evans' visit is?

. . . .

. . . .

9 What does George hope to achieve by contacting Downes?

. . . .

. . . .

10 What does George ask Harry to consider?

. . . .

. . . .

11 What does George feel about his firm's relationship with Bellcrest?

. . . .

. . . .

12 What is Harry's attitude towards this problem?

. . . .

. . . .

ROLE SIMULATION

Statement of Problem

When all his salesmen have returned from visiting customers. Dennis Evans calls them to a meeting together with Tom Driver, the Production Manager. The problem to be discussed concerns the RN1, an electronic component in considerable demand among customers. Unfortunately, the fire destroyed all but 1500 of these components in stock, and the Production Manager maintains that he is unable to produce more than 5000 by the end of next month. The purpose of the meeting is therefore to establish how many RN1's will be required by the end of next month according to existing orders, whether customers are willing to allow their deliveries to be re-scheduled and for Dennis Evans to hear from his salesmen which customers have prior claims on available stocks.

Written follow-up You are Dennis Evans. Write a short report to Paul Malone on the decisions you have made on the basis of your meeting.

DESCRIPTION OF ROLES

Dennis Evans, Sales Manager

You are in the chair at the meeting. Your first priority is to find out from each salesman how many RN1's his customers require, and then to establish whether orders can be re-scheduled. You should proceed to find out from each salesman just how important his most important customer is, bearing in mind the production situation and the fact that you will have to decide on which customers have prior claims on available stocks and inform your salesmen of your decisions.

Tom Driver, Production Manager

Due to damage to your plant installations, you do not feel able to produce more than 5000 RN1's in time for these to be delivered by the end of next month. Bear in mind that if you concentrate your resources on producing more than 5000 RN1's in order to satisfy the salesmen, you will have to cut production of other products.

Salesman

Below are your notes on the most important customer you have just visited. You took the order for Bellcrest, and must bring as much pressure as possible to bear in the meeting to ensure that your customer's requirements are met.

E.C.L. 1750 RN1's ordered. They insist on delivery by the end of next month, or they will buy from Electrovans. They will not re-schedule. Possibility of larger orders to come.

Salesman

Below are your notes on the most important customer you have just visited. You took the order for Bellcrest, and must bring as much pressure as possible to bear in the meeting to ensure that your customer's requirements are met.

W.A.C.I. 1500 RN1's ordered. They can postpone delivery of 1000 for 3 months but by then they will need another 1000. Very large and regular customer.

Salesman

Below are your notes on the most important customer you have just visited. You took the order for Bellcrest, and must bring as much pressure as possible to bear in the meeting to ensure that your customer's requirements are met.
W.T. 2000 RN1's ordered. Delivery due in two weeks. New customer. Will not re-schedule. If the RN1's are not delivered on time, W.T. will turn elsewhere.

Salesman

Below are your notes on the most important customer you have just visited. You took the order for Bellcrest, and must being as much pressure as possible to bear in the meeting to ensure that your customer's requirements are met.
E.I.L. Bellcrest's largest customer. 2500 RN1's on order. Must have at least 1500 by the end of the month. Extremely annoyed at this inconvenience. Present stocks are low.

Salesman

Below are your notes on the most important customer you have just visited. You took the order for Bellcrest, and must bring as much pressure as possible to bear in the meeting to ensure that your customer's requirements are met.

F.A.C. 1500 RN1's ordered. You committed yourself in writing to delivery in ten days. If this date is not kept, F.A.C. will invoke the penalty clauses and discontinue business with Bellcrest. Present stocks exhausted.

Salesman

Below are your notes on the most important customer you have just visited. You took the order for Bellcrest, and must bring as much pressure as possible to bear in the meeting to ensure that your customer's requirements are met.

E.I.I. 750 RN1's ordered. First order from this customer, who previously bought from Electrovans. Possible large orders to come. They want all 750 RN1's within ten days, or they will go back to Electrovans.

Salesman

Below are your notes on the most important customer you have just visited. You took the order for Bellcrest, and must bring as much pressure as possible to bear in the meeting to ensure that your customer's requirements are met.

J.E.I. Bellcrest's second largest customer. 2000 RN1's ordered. Delivery dates to be kept, i.e. by the end of next month.

Salesman

Below are your notes on the most important customer you have just visited. You took the order for Bellcrest,and must bring as much pressure as possible to bear in the meeting to ensure that your customer's requirements are met.

M.I.L. At present they order half their requirements from Bellcrest and the other half from Electrovans. 1000 RN1's on order. They will not re-schedule. Delayed delivery will mean cancellation of the order and loss of business to Electrovans.

A TRIP ABROAD

On his way to visit customers and agents in Europe, Malone unexpectedly ran into Donald Williams, Managing Director of Electrovans, at the air terminal. Williams was also planning to market a speed control device for electric vehicles, similar to the SC1, and had offered a job to Orpenshaw to develop it. Malone told Williams that he knew he had offered Orpenshaw a job. Williams did not attempt to deny it, and added that he thought Orpenshaw should have a chance of continuing his work on the SC1, particularly as he understood that Bellcrest was not interested in the device. When Janet Malone unintentionally revealed that this might not be so, Williams immediately became interested. After Malone had left, he offered Janet a coffee. She accepted, and said she would give him a lift home.

The first customer Malone had to visit was M. Picard in Paris. Bellcrest's inability to deliver on time put Picard in a difficult position. He had persuaded a reluctant Board to order components from a British firm only a short time ago, and to have to admit that these would not be delivered on time would make things very unpleasant both for him and for Bellcrest. Malone had noticed that Picard's order was an extremely large one, and asked him if he really needed a thousand RN2's per month right through the summer. Picard admitted that there was some seasonal variation in his production schedules, but insisted that the transistors he had ordered were needed very urgently indeed. Malone was unable to change his mind on this point.

From Paris Malone flew on to Munich, where he visited some customers and then met Walter Heinlein, Bellcrest's agent in Germany. During the course of their conversation, the question of the SC1 was brought up. Heinlein rather surprisingly wanted to know whether Bellcrest would be willing to sell him the patents in Germany. He said that he thought that there was now a market for an AC speed control device, although there hadn't been five years ago when the SC1 was suspended. Malone was naturally very interested by what Heinlein had to say, and more so when he was told that the D.A.U. company were putting a lot of money into developing a small electric town car. He told Heinlein he would like to follow this up, and Heinlein promised that a meeting would be arranged with D.A.U's Technical Director.

Later that Evening Malone telephoned Janet, who was still worried about speaking out of turn to Donald Williams at the air terminal. When she assured him that she had given away nothing about the SC1 to Williams, Malone told her it didn't matter.

Then next day, Malone visited Dr Lang, Bellcrest's largest customer in Germany. Once again he had to explain the effects of the fire on Bellcrest's delivery schedules and apologize for the inevitable delays. Dr Lang had placed one order which could not be delayed, and that was for a consignment of 4,500 resistors for his model P 43. Although Malone thought it would not be easy to meet this order, he agreed to do what he could.

Dr Lang went on to mention that he had not received his previous consignment of resistors. Heinlein was contacted and he said that the resistors had been in Munich for a week, but had been delayed in the Customs. He added that Dr Lang would receive the resistors that afternoon or the following morning.

Malone then brought up the question of the remainder of Dr Lang's order for the following month, most of which was for components for Dr Lang's AM17 model. Malone found that these were no longer needed, as Dr Lang's company had developed a smaller, cheaper model. These components were, however, exactly those needed by Picard in Paris, so Malone immediately agreed to take 5000 off Dr Lang's hands.

Before he left for Copenhagen, Malone met Heinlein again, who had contacted Picard and arranged to despatch the components to Paris immediately. Heinlein also told Malone that he had been in touch with Dr Mandl, D.A.U.'s Technical Director, and a meeting had been arranged for that afternoon. He had some disturbing news for Malone too. Dr Mandl had told Heinlein that he had had a visitor from another British company, which was developing a speed control device similar to the SC1. Malone guessed that the company was Electrovans and the visitor Donald Williams.

Malone was right. When Williams returned from Europe, he went to Ashburnham's Bank. He promised Sir Frederick that he would send the Bank Electrovans' report on a speed control device the following week. He also told Sir Frederick and Needham that he thought Malone was trying to revive the SC1.

UNIT SUMMARY

Structures **The structures dealt with in this unit are:**

1 Tenses and Time References:

a After 'before, when, until':

We won't be able to make a decision *until* he *comes.*

You will come and see me *before* you *go,* won't you?

b 'Since' contrasted with 'ago':

He has worked for us *since* 1955.

He joined our company twelve years *ago.*

2 Reported Speech:

I'll come and see you tomorrow.

to He said he *would* come and see me tomorrow.

I travel to Europe quite often.

to He said he *travelled* to Europe quite often.

I *am writing* the report.

to He said he *was writing* the report.

3 Formation of the Passive:

a *Present Simple:*

It *is made* in Birmingham.

b *Past Simple:*

It *was built* in 1947.

c *Future Simple:*

The report *will be sent* to you tomorrow.

Vocabulary **The areas of Vocabulary dealt with in this unit are:**

1 Disappointed, grateful etc.

2 Agent, air freight, consignment etc.

ditional Notes **Role Simulation**

The role simulation in this unit involves representatives of two different companies, Bellcrest and The House of Kakubishi, (Japan). It is therefore advisable to extend the role simulation of this unit to include a 'Faction Meeting'. 'Faction Meetings' are dealt with in the Introductory Notes.

COMPREHENSION QUESTIONS

1 When did Malone meet Donald Williams?
2 Who is Donald Williams?
3 Where did Malone meet him?
4 What was Williams intending to do?
5 Was Williams' device the same as the SC1?
6 Why had Williams offered Orpenshaw a job?
7 Did Williams deny offering Orpenshaw a job?
8 What did Williams go on to say?
9 Why particularly did he think this?
10 What was Janet's reaction to what Williams said?

11 What did Williams do after Malone had left?
12 What did Janet offer Williams?
13 Who was the first customer Malone visited?
14 What put Picard in a difficult position?
15 Why did this put Picard in a difficult position?
16 What had Malone noticed about Picard's order?
17 What did Malone ask Picard?
18 How did Picard react?
19 What did Picard insist on?
20 Was Malone able to reach a compromise on the transistors?
21 Where did Malone go after Paris?
22 Who was Heinlein?
23 What did Heinlein want to know about the SC1?
24 Why did he want the patents?
25 Had there been a market for the SC1 when it was suspended?
26 When was it suspended?
27 What made Malone more interested in what Heinlein was saying?
28 What did Malone tell Heinlein when he heard about D.A.U.?
29 What did Heinlein promise Malone?
30 When did Malone phone Janet?
31 What was Janet concerned about?
32 What did she assure Malone of?
33 When did Malone visit Dr Lang?
34 Who is Dr Lang?
35 What did Malone have to explain?
36 How many of Dr Lang's orders could not be delayed?
37 Which order was that?
38 Did Malone foresee difficulties in meeting the order?
39 What did Dr Lang go on to say?
40 What was done about this?
41 When would Dr Lang get his order?
42 What point did Malone then raise?
43 What did this order consist of?
44 Were these components still needed?
45 Why weren't they needed?
46 Who needed these components?
47 Who did Malone see before he went to Copenhagen?
48 What had Heinlein done?
49 What else had Heinlein done?
50 What disturbing news did Heinlein have for Malone?
51 What did Malone think about this?
52 Was Malone's guess right?
53 What did Williams do on his return to U.K.?
54 What did he promise Sir Frederick?
55 What did he also tell the Bank?

EXERCISES

Exercise A

1 When Malone visited Paris he found Picard d. at Bellcrest's inability to deliver according to schedule. Picard a. Bellcrest's difficulties, but as the delay put him in an u. position, he insisted that the components he had ordered were needed u. .H. for Malone, Dr Lang was only too p. to return five thousand of the components Picard needed. This was 1. for Malone, and he was very g. to Dr Lang, as he would have lost Picard's custom if he hadn't been able to meet his order.

2 Malone couldn't understand why Dr Lang's order had been delayed as it had been d. from England by a. f. a month previously. He therefore telephoned his a. , Heinlein. Heinlein told him that the c. had not been c. by Customs, as Bellcrest had not sent sufficient copies of the i. . He also told Malone that he was arranging for Picard's order to be sent on by his f. a. to Paris.

Exercise B *Here are some notes Malone has made reminding him what he will have to do during the day.*

Write full sentences using 'when', 'before' or 'until':

Examples:

Phone Needham – make appointment.
I'll have to make an appointment when I phone Needham.

Adjuster coming – look at policy first
I'll have to look at the policy before the adjuster comes.

Check stock list – delay seeing Driver until then.
I'll have to delay seeing Driver until I check the stock list.

1 Seeing Spence – look though file first.
2 Buyer coming – negotiate contract.
3 Speak Driver – think about production of SC1 first.
4 Lunch with Downes – leave RN2 question until then.
5 Janet phoning – book theatre tickets first.
6 Attend meeting – read agenda first.
7 Ring Urwin – invite to dinner.
8 Write SC1 report – review past developments.
9 Visit M. P. Consultants – brief Evans first.
10 Urwin coming to dinner – keep quiet about Orpenshaw until then.

Exercise C **Complete the sentences from the notes:**

Example:
Picard/informed/Malone/his firm/require a thousand RN2s.
Picard informed Malone that his firm required a thousand RN2s.

1 Urwin/admitted/Malone/he/find Williams very interesting.
2 Spence/warned/the Committee/the Insurance Company/not meet the claim immediately.

3 Malone/explained/Janet/Bellcrest/must keep quiet about the SC1.
4 M.P. Consultants/told/Bellcrest/they think/now a market for the SC1.
5 Spence/pointed out/Downes/the Bank/not know anything about the developmen plans.
6 Janet/mentioned/her husband/Williams/want to find out about the SC1.
7 Evans/assured/his customers/Bellcrest/increase production as soon as possible.
8 Heinlein/informed/Malone/the D.A.U. Company/expanding fast.
9 Orpenshaw/warned/Malone/Electrovans/intend to produce a speed control device.
10 Dr Lang/told/Malone/his firm/not require the ZA24 transistors.

Exercise D Complete these sentences:

Malone: Unfortunately most of our stocks (destroy) last week when a fire (break) out in our factory.

Lang: Yes, I (hear) about it. Several European countries (buy) regularly from Bellcrest and your products (value) in Germany. The fire (report) in our newspapers.

Malone: Some of the reports in the English papers (exaggerate) the extent of the damage. They (not mention) that production (increase) in the near future. Of course, deliveries (delay) to a certain extent.

Lang: Actually, at the moment I am more worried about our last order from Bellcrest. The consignment (expect) about 3 weeks ago but it (fail) to arrive up to now.

Malone: That's very strange. It (air freight) on the second of the month. I (speak) to our agent about it immediately and I hope the matter (settle) to your satisfaction.

Exercise E Written Task

a *You are Paul Malone. Send a telegram to Picard, saying:*

1 His components are being sent immediately from Germany.
2 The forwarding agent is Dupierre of Paris.
3 He will inform Picard of their arrival.
4 He can expect them by the end of the week.
5 A letter is following.

b *Now write the letter to Picard confirming your telegram.*

DRILLS

Drill 1 I'll answer that question but I'm going to speak to Malone first.
OH, I SEE. YOU'RE GOING TO SPEAK TO MALONE BEFORE YOU ANSWER THAT QUESTION.

I'll see Picard soon and then I'll reassure him.
OH, I SEE. YOU'LL REASSURE PICARD WHEN YOU SEE HIM.

Spence is going to write a report, and we'll wait until then.
OH, I SEE. YOU'LL WAIT UNTIL SPENCE WRITES A REPORT.

Drill 2 Oh, I agree it is most unfortunate about the fire.
EVANS AGREED THAT IT WAS MOST UNFORTUNATE ABOUT THE FIRE.

I must admit that Bellcrest won't be able to supply you immediately.
EVANS ADMITTED THAT BELLCREST WOULDN'T BE ABLE TO SUPPLY HIM IMMEDIATELY.

Drill 3 *Malone is showing some visitors round the factory and is answering their questions.*

When did you build this factory?
IT WAS BUILT IN 1957.

Where do you keep your surplus stocks?
THEY ARE KEPT IN OUR WAREHOUSE.

Will you export these goods?
YES, THEY WILL BE EXPORTED TO EUROPE.

1 In 1957
2 In our warehouse
3 To Europe
4 Next week
5 Our Sales Manager

6 Our Chief Engineer
7 All electrically driven vehicles
8 About five years ago

Dialogue **At the Air Terminal**

Paul Malone is returning from Europe. His plane has just landed at Heathrow Airport.

Yes, I am.
Yes, of course.
No, only three days.
Oh, only in Europe. Germany, France and Denmark, actually.
Thank you.
Nothing, actually. I've been on a business trip, not a holiday.
Oh, I see.
No, nothing. I went to the wrong gate, that's all.
No, nothing.

Drill 4 *Malone is talking to Bellcrest's agent in Italy. The agent has a number of requests. Malone thinks these will be difficult to meet. However, he is prepared to offer something.*

I believe we could sell a lot more for you if you would agree to reduce prices by 10%.
IT WOULD BE VERY DIFFICULT TO REDUCE THEM BY 10%, I'M AFRAID, BUT THERE'S A GOOD CHANCE OF REDUCING THEM BY 5%.

1 5%
2 £3,000
3 the end of the month
4 2000 copies
5 2 men
6 10 days
7 the beginning of September
8 a maximum of 20%

Drill 5 *Malone has now telephoned to Downes and told him about the agent's requests. Downes agrees with Malone's reactions.*

Malone is now talking to the agent again and confirming what he said earlier.

I asked if you could reduce prices by 10%.
UNFORTUNATELY WE CAN'T REDUCE THEM BY 10%, BUT ALL BEING WELL, WE SHOULD BE ABLE TO REDUCE THEM BY 5%.

Notice that Malone is still being cautious about what he promises:
'*All being well,* we *should* be able to . . . .'

1 5%
2 £3,000
3 the end of the month
4 2,000 copies
5 2 men
6 10 days
7 the beginning of September
8 a maximum of 20%
9 the end of next week.

ACTIVE LISTENING

During his visit to Germany Malone meets Dr Mandl, the Technical Director of D.A.U. They are discussing their interest in the automotive field.

1 What is the purpose of Malone's visit to Germany?

. . . .

. . . .

2 What has Dr Mandl been working on?

. . . .

. . . .

3 What reason does Mandl give for being interested in this field?

. . . .

. . . .

4 What do both men think will happen before long?

. . . .

. . . .

5 Why does Malone think there are good prospects for electrically driven cars?

. . . .

. . . .

6 What is the main problem in the development of such cars?

. . . .

. . . .

7 What will be the advantage of Bellcrest's device?

. . . .

. . . .

8 Give two reasons why Malone cannot give Mandl more detailed information about the SC1.

. . . .

. . . .

9 Why is Malone so interested in Mandl's reactions, do you think?

. . . .

. . . .

10 What important information does Malone get from Mandl?

. . . .

. . . .

11 Why is Mandl going to London?

. . . .

. . . .

12 Why does Malone want him to visit Bellcrest?

. . . .

ROLE SIMULATION

Statement of Problem

Despite the fire, Bellcrest's work had to go on as normally as was possible in the circumstances. A meeting had been arranged two months before between interested parties in Bellcrest and a visiting Japanese delegation from the House of Kakubishi.

The House of Kakubishi are interested in becoming sole agents in Japan for Bellcrest's RN, BX, HJ, GJ and LX range of components. (The X ranges are transistors, the J ranges are resistors). Japan is a country in which Bellcrest does not yet have an agent. Bellcrest is in principle interested in having an agent in Japan, as they feel there is a potential market of some size for their products in that country.

The Japanese have spent the morning touring Bellcrest and after lunch the two delegations meet to discuss the whole question of the House of Kakubishi's proposed agency for Bellcrest products. It has already been agreed in principle between Downes and Yamaguchi, Managing Director of the House of Kakubishi, that nothing stands in the way of co-operation, subject to other questions being satisfactorily settled. The outstanding problems, among others, to be settled at the meeting are those of deliveries, servicing, product range, or routines, sales literature, advertising, terms and methods of payment and commission.

You should re-enact this meeting.

Written follow-up

Both sides should write a letter confirming the agreements made at the meeting.

DESCRIPTION OF ROLES

Bellcrest

Maurice Downes

You are keen to get the House of Kakubishi to agree to become your agent on the most favourable terms you can get. You want to start by offering them the BX and RN range of components and seeing whether they can sell those before you commit yourself to any large-scale business with them. You are in the chair at the meeting. You are free to invent such facts as are necessary to your role. At the meeting you are cautious, and particularly want to find out as much as possible about the House of Kakubishi, including the size of the company, the number of employees and warehouse facilities.

Paul Malone

You are very eager to expand into the Japanese market, as you see good prospects of selling the SC1 there. You are primarily concerned with questions of product range, sales literature and advertising. You would like to see the House of Kakubishi launch a large sales campaign on behalf of Bellcrest products with massive advertising to back it up.

Tom Driver

You are concerned with questions of supply. The Japanese will certainly want to know how many of the various products you can produce in any one month. You are free to invent such facts as may be necessary.

Charles Spence

You are concerned with the terms and methods of payment to be employed, and with the agents' commission and prices. You should enquire closely into the House of Kakubishi's financial affairs. You may invent such facts as may be necessary.

Dennis Evans

You are concerned with servicing and order routines. You should be prepared to tell the House of Kakubishi what service facilities you are able to offer, and routines they should follow when ordering from you. You are free to invent such facts as may be necessary.

Secretary

Your job is to keep the minutes of the meeting and to give a summary of the agreements made at the end. You are a little deaf, and so often need to have things repeated.

The House of Kakubishi

Yamaguchi

You are the Managing Director of the company. You are keen to settle on the terms of your agency as soon as possible. You want the complete range of Bellcrest Products. You are particularly concerned with terms and methods of payment, and with your commission. Try to get the best possible deal out of Bellcrest. You are free to invent such facts about your company and the Japanese market as may be necessary.

Yamakawa

You are the Marketing Manager of your company. You are convinced you can make a handsome profit by selling Bellcrest products in Japan. You should naturally try to get the products as cheaply as possible from Bellcrest. You are particularly concerned with the product range, sales literature and advertising. You want Bellcrest to pay the costs of any advertising or sales campaign. You are free to invent such facts about your company and the Japanese market as may be necessary.

Suzuki

You are the Sales Manager of your company. You are particularly concerned with the service facilities Bellcrest can offer you and their order routines. You are free to invent such facts about your company and the market in Japan as may be necessary.

Sato

You are the Supply Manager of your company. You are particularly concerned with deliveries and transport. You are free to invent your monthly requirements of Bellcrest products, and any other facts about your company as may be necessary.

EPISODE 9 STUDYING THE MARKET

After Donald Williams' visit to the Bank, Sir Frederick and Needham discussed whether to support Bellcrest or Electrovans. Needham felt that Electrovans was more adventurous than Bellcrest. Sir Frederick agreed with this, but felt that Bellcrest was sounder than Electrovans. He pointed out that Electrovans was still very dependent on one or two big customers: 45% of Electrovans' business went to one company, Beamish Motors, for example. Needham had to agree with this, although he still believed that Electrovans was more forward-looking than Bellcrest. Sir Frederick, however, was not prepared to make up his mind which company to invest in.

Malone returned from Europe and reported back to Downes. Downes was not at all happy about Dr Mandl's visit to Bellcrest, in spite of the fact that D.A.U. represented a potential customer for the SC1. Malone pointed out that although D.A.U. was only a potential customer, this was the first direct contact Bellcrest had had with a vehicle manufacturer. He felt that this was a great opportunity which should not be overlooked. Downes conceded the point as it was too late to put Dr Mandl off.

Downes went on to tell Malone that there was to be a Board meeting in ten days' time, and that the SC1 was bound to be mentioned. Although there wasn't time enough to circulate a complete report before the meeting, he wanted as much information from the market survey as possible.

Malone went at once to Orpenshaw, who at first didn't want to see him or any visitors, as he had a lot of work to do on the SC1. Malone reminded him that Dr Mandl was coming. Orpenshaw was quite happy to see Dr Mandl, as he felt that Mandl would be more interested in the SC1 as a piece of engineering than anyone else. Malone asked him whether he had any test results ready, and told him that he needed as much information as possible in three days' time. Orpenshaw was disgusted at only having three days, but said he would do what he could.

When Dr Mandl arrived, Malone introduced him to Orpenshaw, who got on extremely well with him. Orpenshaw was careful to explain only what the SC1 did, not how it worked, and Dr Mandl had plenty of questions to ask him. When, at the end of his visit, Orpenshaw took Dr Mandl to see Downes, he said he liked the SC1 very much. Although he said Orpenshaw had asked him more questions than he had asked Orpenshaw, he told Downes that he had learned all he needed to know about the SC1. He had thought of visiting another company to discuss speed controls, but that would no longer be necessary.

Although he would have preferred to stay with Dr Mandl, Malone had to go up to London with Evans to see M.P. Consultants and hear the results of their preliminary study.

M.P. Consultants hadn't really had enough time to prepare their study. When Malone arrived, Sherwood and Dean, Dr Perkins' assistants, started to run through the data they had collected. They showed him some statistics on a screen, including a chart showing the growth in production over the past twenty years: total electric vehicle production had risen from 3,450 to 18,000 a year during this period. Malone interrupted to say that as all this information was contained in their report he would prefer not to go through it now but concentrate on details that affected the SC1.

Sherwood and Dean were not able to give him much detailed information. They had found out that most electronic control systems at present in use were fairly simple, whereas the SC1 was not. They had sent questionnaires to vehicle manufacturers, who indicated that the SC1 would only be of interest to them if it enabled them to offer a more attractive product for their customers to buy than their present power systems. They had also questioned the customers, and their research indicated that 55% would welcome the increased mileage a device like the SC1 would offer, as long as there was no increase in cost to achieve it, whereas only 25% felt that increased mileage was worth paying for. These findings were not particularly encouraging for Malone.

Dr Perkins added that they had also questioned potential users of electric vehicles but, to Malone's disappointment, had only had time to include some of their preliminary findings in their report.

Dr Perkins went on to discuss car manufacturers, most of whom seemed to be more aware of the disadvantages of battery-driven cars than of the advantages. All car manufacturers were agreed on the requirements of small cars for cities. These were small size, simple operation, good manoeuvrability, minimum pollution and low cost. Malone pointed out that an electric car suited these requirements and that the SC1 went a long way towards solving one of its main drawbacks: its short range. Dr Perkins said they hoped to cover the smaller manufacturers more thoroughly in the next stage of their research, as at the moment they only had rumours, not hard facts. She mentioned a rumour that Cremorne Cars had already thought of developing an electric city car, but had dropped the project as they had not been able to persuade an electronics firm to develop the right kind of speed control. Cremorne Cars had refused to confirm the rumour, and their name was not mentioned in M.P. Consultants' report. Malone asked Dr Perkins to take the matter up with them again without mentioning Bellcrest's name.

Electrovans had by now submitted their report on their AC speed control to Ashburnham's Bank. Sir Frederick was impressed by the report, but despite Needham's enthusiasm for Electrovans he insisted on waiting for Bellcrest's report before making any decision about the Bank's loan.

UNIT SUMMARY

Structures The structures dealt with in this unit are:

1 Adjectives: comparative with 'than' :

The SC1 is *better than* Electrovans' device.

2 Much, Many, A lot of, More:

He hasn't got *much* work.
We don't have *many* visitors in the summer.
There is still *a lot of* work to do.

3 Connectives: Although, In spite of, While, Whereas:

Evans visited U.K. customers *while* Malone went to Europe.
In spite of the difficulties involved, Malone pushed ahead with the SC1.
Although he had management support, Malone still had to convince the Board.
Downes is cautious, *whereas* Williams is adventurous.

Vocabulary The areas of vocabulary dealt with in this unit are:

1 Adventurous/forward-looking etc.
2 Statistics and data.

Additional Notes **Drill 3** This is a drill on numbers.

Role Simulation
The role simulation in this unit involves representatives of two different companies, Bellcrest and D.A.U. It is therefore advisable to extend the role simulation of this. unit to include a 'Faction Meeting' . 'Faction Meetings' are dealt with in the Introductory Notes.

COMPREHENSION QUESTIONS

1 What did Sir Frederick and Needham discuss?
2 When did they discuss it?
3 Which company did Needham think was more adventurous?
4 Which company did Sir Frederick think was sounder?
5 Why did he think this?
6 Which company did Needham think was more forward-looking?
7 Did Sir Frederick decide which company to invest in?
8 Was Downes pleased to hear about Dr Mandl's visit?
9 Why was Malone so keen on Dr Mandl's visit?
10 Why did Downes allow Dr Mandl to visit Bellcrest?
11 When was the next Board meeting?
12 Why did Downes mention this?
13 What did Downes want before the Board meeting?
14 Why didn't Orpenshaw want to see any visitors?
15 What did Orpenshaw feel about Dr Mandl's visit?

16 Why?
17 What did Malone ask him?
18 When did Malone need the information?
19 What was Orpenshaw's reaction to this?
20 Did Orpenshaw like Dr Mandl?
21 What did Orpenshaw tell Dr Mandl about the SC1?
22 What did Dr Mandl think of the SC1?
23 How much had Dr Mandl found out about the SC1?
24 Where did Malone have to go?
25 Did he want to do this?
26 What was covered in M.P. Consultants' preliminary report?
27 What information was missing?
28 Why was this?
29 What statistics did Sherwood and Dean show Malone?
30 Why did Malone not want to go through this data at that point?
31 What did Malone want to discuss instead?
32 What information did Sherwood and Dean have on control systems?
33 How had they found this out?
34 What had the manufacturers said about the speed controls?
35 Who else had M.P. Consultants questioned?
36 What did their answers indicate?
37 Did the findings encourage Malone?
38 What did Dr Perkins say was uppermost in car manufacturers' minds?
39 What did car manufacturers agree on?
40 Did an electric car meet these requirements?
41 What role would the SC1 play in meeting these requirements?
42 When would Dr Perkins cover smaller manufacturers?
43 Why?
44 What project had Cremorne Cars thought of working on?
45 Why did they drop it?
46 Were Cremorne Cars willing to confirm their interest?
47 What was Malone's reaction?
48 How did Sir Frederick react to the Electrovans report?

EXERCISES

Exercise A **Complete the following sentences:**

1 Ashburnham and Needham discussed whether to support Bellcrest or Electrovans. Needham felt that Electrovans were more a. than Bellcrest, and that the company was a f. -l. concern. Williams, he said, had p. a. with development whereas Downes had been more cautious. Sir Frederick felt that Electrovans l. the s. of Bellcrest and were too d. on one or two large customers. Needham replied that that was the reason why Williams wanted capital to b. f. and f. e. . Without this capital, he couldn't a. to.

2 When Malone visited M.P. Consultants he was shown some s on the d. Sherwood and Dean had collected. The s. showed the principal manufacturers of electric vehicles and their v. of p. .Malone was shown a c. on a screen indicating the g. in production and the t. p. of electric vehicles over the past twenty years. To get this information, M.P. Consultants had sent q. to vehicle manufacturers. A lot of the data on potential customers was not included in their p. s. , as the p. f. were outside its s. .

Exercise B **Write sentences from the following notes:**

Examples:
Make/our own enquiries/cheap/commission a survey.
Making our own enquiries is cheaper than commissioning a survey.

Develop/project/interesting/sell/products.
Developing a project is more interesting than selling products.

1 Live/home/comfortable/stay/second-rate hotel.
2 Pay/high insurance premium/good/lose/a lot/money.
3 Make/statement/simple/give interviews.
4 Meet/orders/satisfactory/ask/customers/accept delays.
5 Soak/papers/water/bad/burn/them.
6 Make/components/ourselves/expensive/buy/Bellcrest.
7 Finance/new developments/progressive/look for/quick profits.
8 Find/markets/hard/plan/production.
9 Approach/potential customers/adventurous/wait/them/approach/us.
10 Commission/survey/safe/listen/rumours.

Exercise C **Complete the sentences using 'much', 'many', 'a lot of' and 'more':**

Perkins: We sent out questionnaires to firms that already use electric vehicles.

Malone: Did of them reply?

Perkins: About 40%, which is quite compared with other surveys. than half of these companies felt that there would not be advantage in increased mileage if this raised the cost of the vehicle. Only 25% of them felt it would be worth paying for increased mileage.

Malone: 25%! That's not

Perkins: I'm afraid we haven't been able to find out about potential users of electric vehicles although we questioned companies in the private vehicle sector. There seems to be interest abroad than in the U.K. I think you would get quite support from European companies. But at the moment there are not British manufacturers interested in developing an electric car. Of course there have been rumours that Cremorne Cars tried to develop an electric city car but dropped the project because they couldn't get the right kind of AC speed control. Unfortunately, they won't confirm these rumours, so we haven't to go on in the way of hard facts. However, we will try to get information about this.

Exercise D *Sir Frederick and Needham are discussing whether to support Bellcrest or Electrovans.*

Complete the following sentences, using 'while', 'although', 'in spite of' and 'whereas':

Example:
Needham didn't like Downes, although *he admitted he was a good businessman.*

Sir Frederick: Downes is a sound businessman his reluctance to take risks. I know he abandoned a lot of development projects getting Bellcrest back on its feet again, but this was necessary if the company was to remain in business. And he did a very good job, forcing Williams to resign was perhaps a mistake. Downes has increased profits still maintaining a high level of technical excellence. Bellcrest sell to a wide range of customers Electrovans is still very dependent on one company for their trade.

Needham: Well, Sir Frederick, I agree wholeheartedly with what you say, I think you have perhaps overlooked one or two points. Williams has the full backing of his staff Downes has lost the support of some of his technical staff. Men like Orpenshaw don't like to see their projects abandoned even they may appreciate the financial reasons for such measures. In fact it is quite possible that Orpenshaw may transfer to Electrovans this has not been settled yet. If he leaves Bellcrest, the company will find it difficult to develop this speed control having produced the original designs.

Exercise E Written Task

Cremorne Cars was one of the manufacturers that received a questionnaire from M. P. Consultants. The Managing Director of the company, K.C.Y., passed this on to his Marketing Manager, D.B., with an accompanying memo. Write this memo for him. Use these notes:

just received
to our advantage to fill it in
draw your attention Question 6
advantages of AC speed control?
which firm has commissioned this survey?

DRILLS

Drill 1 We're getting the research done by management consultants but I don't know how quick they are.
GETTING THE RESEARCH DONE BY MANAGEMENT CONSULTANTS IS QUICKER THAN DOING IT OURSELVES, DON'T YOU THINK?

We must increase production of the BX10 and I don't know how difficult this is.
INCREASING PRODUCTION OF THE BX10 IS MORE DIFFICULT THAN RESCHEDULING THE ORDERS, DON'T YOU THINK?

I've received a little information but I don't know how good it is.
RECEIVING A LITTLE INFORMATION IS BETTER THAN RECEIVING NONE, DON'T YOU THINK?

1 quick/do/it/ourselves
2 difficult/reschedule/orders
3 good/receive/none
4 important/listen/rumours
5 easy/persuade/Bank/extend/loan
6 urgent/go on with/technical developments
7 bad/damage/warehouse
8 appropriate/concern/ourselves/ industrial sector

Drill 2 Do you do any business with French companies?
NO, NOT MUCH REALLY, BUT WE DO A LOT OF BUSINESS WITH GERMAN COMPANIES.

Have you any contacts in Norway?
NO, NOT MANY REALLY, BUT WE HAVE A LOT OF CONTACTS IN SWEDEN.

1 German companies
2 Sweden
3 petrochemicals
4 surge diverters
5 research and development
6 prices
7 labour
8 industrial vehicle sector

Drill 3 60% of our customers are completely satisfied.
DOES THAT MEAN THAT 40% OF THEM ARE COMPLETEY DISSATISFIED?

Two thirds of the directors supported the project.
DOES THAT MEAN THAT ONE THIRD OF THEM OPPOSED IT?

Dialogue **At the Air Terminal.**
Dr Mandl is flying back from Heathrow to Munich.

I'm on flight 642 to Munich. This is the right check-in desk, isn't it?
Yes, one minute. Ah, here we are.
I give that up at the departure gate, don't I?
Yes, this overnight case and a briefcase.
Not at all. They're not overweight, I hope.
Yes, here it is.
No, only a few days, actually.
Oh, of course. There we are.
Oh, yes. One minute, it's locked. I've got the key here. Here it is.
My overcoat?
Oh, I see.
Thank you very much.

Drill 4 *Dr Mary Perkins of M.P. Consultants, and Brian Dean, her assistant, are discussing the advantages of electric city cars and of the SC1.*

Of course, electricity is cheap.
YES, IT CERTAINLY *IS* CHEAP, AND WHAT'S MORE, IT'S AVAILABLE EVERYWHERE.

1 available everywhere
2 easy to park
3 quiet
4 easier to drive
5 cheap to service
6 increases battery life
7 not heavy
8 time for lunc

Drill 5 *Paul Malone is at M.P. Consultants. Jim Sherwood is talking about the preliminary market study. Malone feels the information is too general. He keeps interrupting and asking for more specific information. He is rather annoyed.*

Our investigations show that the market for electric vehicles is growing, and . . .

EXCUSE ME, MR. SHERWOOD. WE *KNOW* THAT THE MARKET FOR ELECTRIC VEHICLES IS GROWING. WHAT WE WANT TO KNOW IS *HOW FAST* IT'S GROWING.

1 how fast?
2 by whom?
3 how much?
4 by whom?
5 *which* airports?
6 how many?
7 *how* soon?
8 when?

ACTIVE LISTENING

The Managing Director and the Marketing Manager of Cremorne Cars are discussing a letter they have received from M.P. Consultants.

1 What do M. P. Consultants want?

. . . .

. . . .

2 How had they dealt with the first letter?

. . . .

. . . .

3 What is Fred's reaction to this letter?

. . . .

. . . .

4 Why would Cremorne Cars be interested in the development of an AC speed control?

. . . .

. . . .

5 What reasons does Fred give for thinking that the enquiry does not originate from Bellcrest?

. . . .

. . . .

6 What does Fred think of Downes?

. . . .

. . . .

7 Who does Fred think must be employing the consultants?

. . . .

. . . .

8 If his guess is correct, why would this be bad for Cremorne Cars?

. . . .

. . . .

9 Why can't they find out if their guess is correct?

. . . .

. . . .

10 What does the Managing Director decide to do?

. . . .

. . . .

11 Why will the Managing Director write a covering letter?

. . . .

. . . .

12 What does Fred suggest that they should do?

. . . .

. . . .

ROLE SIMULATION

Statement of Problem

When Dr Mandl returned to D.A.U. in Germany he submitted an extremely enthusiastic report on the SC1, strongly recommending that it be used in D.A.U.'s projected electric vehicles. He managed to convince his Managing Director to buy from Bellcrest and shortly afterwards four representatives of D.A.U. arrived in Leicester with a view to enquiring as to Bellcrest's production plans and schedules and obtaining an estimate.

As D.A.U. propose to start manufacturing their electric vehicles within a year, they are naturally anxious to tie Bellcrest down to delivery dates and quantities as far as is possible.

The D.A.U. representatives arrived in England last night, and today they are to come to Bellcrest. Re-enact their meeting.

Written follow-up

Write a letter to either Bellcrest or D.A.U. confirming any agreements or proposals made at the meeting.

DESCRIPTION OF ROLES

Bellcrest **Maurice Downes**

Despite D.A.U.'s and Paul Malone's enthusiasm, you are still sceptical as to the chances of your Board approving production of the SC1. You are therefore very reluctant to make any firm commitment to D.A.U. but at the same time you do not want to lose an extremely important potential customer. You should draw up an agenda for the meeting, which you didn't really want. Malone invited the D.A.U. representatives without consulting you, and you are annoyed about that.

Bob Orpenshaw

You are present in order to answer any technical questions that may arise. You have already told Dr Mandl everything that you are willing to say about how the SC1 works, though you are prepared to say more about what it does. You should be prepared to tell D.A.U. how many weeks, or months of development and testing you still have to do before production can start.

Tom Driver

You should be prepared to tell D.A.U. how long it will take you to set up a production line for the SC1, and how many you would be able to produce in a month. You are also responsible for telling them when deliveries could start.

Charles Spence

You are responsible for costing the SC1, and should be prepared to quote D.A.U. a price. You should also be prepared to answer questions about possible discounts and methods of payment. You are free to dictate these terms, or negotiate as you wish. You are worried about making any commitment to D.A.U. before the Board approves the project. You really want D.A.U. to negotiate with Heinlein, your agent in Germany.

Paul Malone

You arranged the meeting without consulting anyone else at Bellcrest because you think that if you can get a firm order for the SC1 out of D.A.U. you will be in a position to force the Board to approve the project. Reluctantly your colleagues have agreed to attend the meeting. You are not empowered to make an agreement with D.A.U. yourself, but must get Downes' and Spence's approval first. You are particularly anxious to find out how many SC1's D.A.U. will require per month and to explore other possibilities of doing business with them.

Secretary

Your job is to keep the minutes of the meeting and to give a summary of agreements and proposals made at the end.

D.A.U. **Hans Schumann**

You are the Production Manager of D.A.U. and are therefore the senior representative of your company. Your instructions are to get as many firm commitments out of Bellcrest as possible. You are convinced that the SC1 is going to be the best speed control on the market, and are therefore very anxious to stake your claim on what Bellcrest will be able to produce. You are not interested in Bellcrest's internal politics, but assume that their Board will approve the project. You should prepare exactly what commitments you intend to get out of Bellcrest, and you cannot go back to Germany until you have got them.

Supply Manager (Peter Neumann)
You are responsible for knowing exactly how many SC1's you will require per month, and when deliveries should start. You want to be able to order direct from Bellcrest, not through their agent in Germany, Heinlein, as you personally dislike him.

Assistant to the Financial Director (Karl Schmidt)
You are responsible for negotiating the price of the SC1. You should argue for a discount for regular, guaranteed orders. You are also responsible for the methods of payment. As it will be cheaper to order direct from Bellcrest, you do not want to do business witb Bellcrest's agent, Heinlein.

Technical Director (Dr Mandl)
You have to discuss any further technical questions there may be with Orpenshaw. You really want to find out from him how the SC1 works. You should also be prepared to argue about the length of time Orpenshaw wants for further development and testing. Remember Heinlein gave you the Bellcrest contact.

AGENDA AND MINUTES

Ashburnham had still not made up his mind whether to support Electrovans or Bellcrest. He had discussed the question with Needham. All relevant. information on their project had already been sent by Electrovans, but nothing definite had been heard from Bellcrest. All the information on the SC1 that was available had been supplied by Donald Williams. Ashburnham therefore decided to telephone Downes himself with a view to finding out what Bellcrest's plans were.

When Sir Frederick rang, Downes was most unwilling to reveal anything. Sir Frederick said he was prepared to extend Bellcrest's deadline by a month, although it would be useful to have some information before then. Downes answered that both the Bank and the Board of Directors would be given full details as soon as they became available. The next Board meeting was in a week's time, and the Bank's loan would certainly be discussed. Sir Frederick was obliged to accept this and Downes had succeeded in revealing nothing about the SC1. When Downes rang off, Needham said that at least the question of the Bank's loan would be on the agenda of the next Board meeting and that this might help him in getting more information about the SC1.

When Downes had finished talking to Sir Frederick, he rang up Paul Malone about the market study from M.P. Consultants. He told Malone he didn't like it, as he didn't think the findings would persuade the Board of Directors to back the SC1. Malone protested that the study only showed the preliminary findings and that the general picture was much brighter. He mentioned D.A.U. and Cremorne Cars as potential customers, but Downes dismissed these as rumours, not hard facts. Malone said he would see whether he could get any definite information about Cremorne Cars' interest and would let Downes know.

Malone immediately rang up Dr Perkins, but she was unable to supply any further information, at least none that could be put on paper. Malone was extremely disappointed. When Downes heard this, he said that the SC1 could not now be discussed at the next Board meeting as the case for backing the SC1 was not good enough. He told Malone to get his report ready for circulation by the 20th August instead.

At that point Spence came in to show Downes the revised agenda for the coming Board meeting. Spence was surprised to hear that Downes no longer wanted to discuss the SC1 at the meeting. In order to avoid giving Needham any chance of bringing up the subject, Downes changed the wording of item four on the agenda from 'To consider development projects in connection with the loan from Ashburnham's Bank' to 'To consider suggested repayment of the Ashburnham Bank loan'. Spence wondered whether Downes was not being overcautious, because as far as they both knew, Needham was unaware of the proposal to revive the SC1. Downes felt, however, that if he was given the chance Needham would press for details of the project and suggested that Spence should look up the minutes of the meeting at which the SC1 was suspended five years before.

At the Board meeting, Downes stated that the Company could not afford to lose the Bank's support. The Bank's position was confirmed by Needham, who said that the loan would only be continued if Bellcrest showed evidence of worthwhile development projects. Downes admitted that a major project was being considered, but declined to go into details. Needham, then said that it was rumoured that Bellcrest was thinking of reviving the SC1, a project that had been axed five years before.

Downes replied that he was concerned that a Director had heard a rumour and had failed to inform the management of the company. He asked Needham to have a word with him about the source of the rumour after the meeting. He was forced, however, to admit that the SC1 was being considered for development, but said that a full report would not be tabled until the next Board meeting.

Needham persisted. He asked why revival of the SC1 was necessary when it had been rejected five years before. Downes replied that it had been suspended, not rejected, and Spence confirmed this by looking up the minutes of the Board meeting of 3rd March, 1966. Unfortunately, March, one of the Directors, remembered the sentence that followed this in the minutes, which said that it had been resolved that the possibility of selling the patents and designs to another company should be considered. The discussion was continued.

After the meeting Downes had a word with Needham. He told Needham that he knew the Bank didn't like having to wait another month for a full discussion on development plans, but that he always insisted on decisions being taken on the basis of adequate information. Adequate information on the SC1 was not yet to hand. He went on to ask Needham where he had picked up the rumour that the SC1 was being revived, to which Needham replied that the wife of one of his senior executives had been rather indiscreet. Downes assumed this was Janet Malone and told Paul Malone.

On their way to the theatre that evening, Paul Malone brought this up with his wife. Janet angrily insisted that she did not know Needham. She suggested that Donald Williams might have told Needham. When Malone refused to believe this, she lost her temper, got out of the car and went home.

UNIT SUMMARY

Structures **The Structures dealt with in this unit are:**

1 The Passive:
The forms of the Present and Past Continuous, Present and Past Perfect.

The study *is being prepared* by M. P. Consultants.
A speed control device *was being developed* by Electrovans.
The agenda *has been circulated* to all Board members.
The warehouse *had been destroyed* by the fire.

2 Impersonals:
The Passive used in formal situations, e.g. Board Meetings.

It was decided to suspend the SC1.

3 Infinitive v. Gerund:

Malone went to Germany *with a view to seeing* Heinlein.
It was *resolved to abandon* negotiations.

Vocabulary **The areas of vocabulary dealt with in this unit are:**

1 Persuasion and Conviction.
2 Vocabulary for meetings.

dditional Notes **Dialogue**

This dialogue has three phases. The first two phases are exactly the same as those in the previous unit (repetition and role-play). In the third phase the pupil is required to select which expression he is going to use from the alternatives given on the page. It is advisable to point out the existence of the alternatives before starting the dialogue.

COMPREHENSION QUESTIONS

1 Had Sir Frederick made a decision or not?
2 What had been sent to the Bank by Electrovans?
3 What had been received from Bellcrest?
4 Who had supplied the Bank's information on the SC1?
5 What did Ashburnham decide?
6 Why did he do this?
7 Was Downes happy to tell Sir Frederick about the SC1?
8 How much extra time was the Bank willing to give Bellcrest?
9 When would Downes give the Bank details of the SC1?
10 Was Downes going to give these details only to the Bank?
11 When was the next Board meeting?
12 What would be discussed at it?
13 What had Downes succeeded in doing?
14 What comfort did Needham get from this conversation?
15 Why would this help him?

16 Why didn't Downes like the preliminary study done by M. P. Consultants?
17 What was Malone's reaction to this?
18 What examples did Malone give Downes?
19 What did Downes think of these examples?
20 What was Malone's reaction to this?
21 What kind of information on Cremorne Cars could Dr Perkins give Malone?
22 What was Downes' reaction to what Dr Perkins said;
23 Why didn't Downes want to discuss the SC1 at the Board meeting?
24 What did Downes tell Malone to do?
25 Why did Spence want to see Downes?
26 Why did Downes change the wording of item four on the agenda?
27 Why did Spence think Downes was being too cautious?
28 What did Downes think Needham would do at the meeting?
29 What did he suggest Spence should do?
30 What was the Bank's position on the loan?
31 What did Downes say about development projects?
32 What subject did Needham then raise?
33 How did Downes handle this?
34 What did Downes have to admit?
35 When did Downes say details of the SC1 would be available?
36 Did Needham try to continue discussing the SC1?
37 What did Needham say?
38 What was Downes' answer?
39 How did Spence confirm this?
40 What did the following sentence in the minutes say?
41 On what basis did Downes tell Needham he took decisions?
42 Was this kind of information on the SC1 available?
43 How did Needham say he had heard about the SC1?
44 What conclusion did Downes jump to?
45 When did Malone bring this up with Janet?
46 What did Janet answer?
47 Who did Janet suggest might have told Needham?
48 Did Malone believe this?
49 What was Janet's reaction?

EXERCISES

Exercise A **Complete the following sentences:**

1 Downes told Malone that the findings of the preliminary survey did not s. him. As the findings did not c. him, he felt that the study would not be enough to p. the Board to back the SC1. He said he needed h. f. to p. to the Board, not r. . He added that the facts and figures in the survey were not s. on their own, and asked Malone to prepare a full report for c. by 20th August.

2 Spence brought the a. for the next Board meeting in to Downes. As Downes didn't want to discuss the SC1, the w. of i. four had to be r. . Downes did this so that Needham would have no chance of r. the s. of the SC1, and pressing for d. of the project. He also told Spence to look up the m. of the meeting at which the SC1 had been suspended in case he was unable to keep Needham off the s. of development projects.

3 When Needham raised the subject of the SC1 at the Board meeting, Downes confirmed that a major project was u. c. . He said he intended to s. his management's r. at the next Board meeting, when he hoped to be able to t. a full r. on the project. A more important i. to Downes was the source of the rumour Needham had heard.

4 Downes told Needham that the SC1 had been suspended five years before, not rejected, and Spence confirmed this by looking up the r. m. . Mr. March said, however, that Spence was q. parts of a document o. of c. as the following sentence recommended that the patents and designs should be sold.

Exercise B **Complete these sentences:**

When Downes realized that Bellcrest's loan (reconsider) by the Bank, he called a meeting of the management committee to discuss plans for diversification. The SC1 (choose) as the most promising new product. This device (invent) by Bob Orpenshaw several years before but the project (suspend) because of financial difficulties. There had been quite a controversy over the matter and Donald Williams, the Marketing Manager, (oblige) to resign because of it. Downes did not want to reveal Bellcrest's renewed interest in the SC1 until a market survey (carry out) by a firm of management consultants.

At the moment, this study (conduct) by M.P. Consultants. A preliminary survey (just complete) from the answers to questionnaires which (send out) some weeks previously. Downes (now see) this survey. He found it disappointing and decided not to mention the SC1 to the Board of Directors, although he (continually press) by the Bank to give them details of his development plans. M. P. Consultants (ask) to investigate rumours that Cremorne Cars are interested in manufacturing an electric car, and at the moment further enquiries (make)

Exercise C *These are some of the notes Miss Armstrong took at the last Board meeting.* **Using these notes, write complete sentences as they would appear in the minutes. Follow the pattern given in the example:**

decide/suspend/SC1.

It was decided *to suspend the SC1.*

1 Resolve/abandon/work/BX10.
2 Suggest/all development projects/review.
3 Decide/postpone/discussion/SC1/next meeting.
4 Assume/full report/ready/August 20th.
5 The Chairman/request/table/full report/SC1.
6 SC1/consider/too expensive.
7 Increase/Directors' fees/approve.
8 The Directors/request/be/more punctual.
9 Resolve/diversify/product range/within the near future.
10 Next meeting/arrange/September 2nd.

Exercise D **Complete the sentences:**

Examples:

Downes did not want to go to the trouble (inform) the Board.
Downes did not want to go to the trouble of informing the Board.

He was unwilling (raise) the matter.
He was unwilling to raise the matter.

Bellcrest had revived the SC1 project with a view (diversify) their product range. Electrovans were also interested (market) a speed control device similar to the SC1. Both companies were eager (get) financial support from Ashburnham's Bank. Donald Williams, the Managing Director of Electrovans, had already drawn up proposals (develop) his product and he took every opportunity (present) his case to Sir Frederick Ashburnham. Maurice Downes, on the other hand, insisted (treat) Bellcrest's project as confidential. He maintained that there was no point (discuss) the plans until detailed information was available. Sir Frederick was unwilling (decide) which firm to support. His assistant, Edward Needham, thought there was a good case (invest) in Electrovans and he persisted (draw) Sir Frederick's attention to the advantages (support) Williams. However, Sir Frederick was not prepared (commit) himself.

Exercise E **Written Task**

Charles Spence has to send out letters to members of the Board confirming arrangements for the next meeting. Minutes of the previous meeting and agenda are also enclosed. Write this letter for Spence. Use these notes:

1 time, date and place of next meeting.
2 enclosures.
3 agenda.
4 of special importance: renewal of bank loan.

DRILLS

Drill 1 *Two executives from a motor manufacturer's are discussing recent developments in the automotive field.*

Was Donald Williams trying to find out about Bellcrest?
YES, BUT HE WASN'T THE ONLY ONE. QUESTIONS WERE BEING ASKED BY EDWARD NEEDHAM AS WELL.

Are Bellcrest working on an AC speed control?
YES, BUT THEY AREN'T THE ONLY ONES. THAT DEVICE IS BEING DEVELOPED BY ELECTROVANS AS WELL.

1 questions/ask/Edward Needham
2 that device/develop/Electrovans
3 interest/show/private vehicle sector
4 electric cars/design/British firm
5 potential users/question/consultants
6 the market/study/Electrovans
7 a contract/negotiate/Passlee Electronics
8 Williams' proposals/considered/Sir Frederick

Drill 2 *Sir Keith Frisby, a member of Bellcrest's Board of Directors, was absent from a meeting of the Board. After the meeting he rings Downes to ask him what was decided.*

Did you decide anything about new projects?
YES, IT WAS DECIDED TO REVIEW NEW PROJECTS.

And the SC1? Did you resolve to continue with it?
NO, IT WAS RESOLVED THAT THE SC1 SHOULD BE SUSPENDED.

1 yes/decided/to/review
2 no/resolved/that/suspended
3 no/suggested/that/abandoned
4 no/proposed/that/not/sold
5 no/decided/not/to abandon/completely
6 yes/suggested/that/maintained
7 no/proposed/that/continue
8 yes/agreed/that/approached

Drill 3 *Malone is talking to Orpenshaw about the problem of support for the SC1.*

The Bank may finance Electrovans. Needham considers it has a case.
I SEE. NEEDHAM CONSIDERS THE BANK HAS A CASE FOR FINANCING ELECTROVANS.

Downes isn't giving them any information. He's very unwilling.
I SEE. HE'S VERY UNWILLING TO GIVE THEM ANY INFORMATION.

Dialogue **Asking for information**

Paul Malone rings up Dr Perkins to ask for more information on potential customers.

HELLO	DR PERKINS? Is that Dr Perkins?

I WANTED TO	TAKE UP	THE
I wonder if I could	raise	
I'd like to		

MATTER OF CREMORNE CARS.	IS IT POSSIBLE TO
question	Can you
	Are you able to
	Are you in a position to

GIVE ME	ANY MORE INFORMATION?	I REALLY DO NEED
let me have	further	I'm very anxious to get

SOME	HARD	FACTS	TO PRESENT TO	MY	BOARD.
	concrete	information	to put before		
	reliable				

THAT'S A PITY.
That's very unfortunate.
That's rather awkward.

I QUITE UNDERSTAND.
Yes, I see your point.

I'D BE MOST GRATEFUL / I'd appreciate it — IF YOU COULD.

NOT AT THE MOMENT, / Not just now, — THANK YOU. GOODBYE, DR PERKINS.

Drill 4 *Maurice Downes and Charles Spence are talking informally in Downes's office. Notice how Spence 'picks up' a subject mentioned by Downes, in order to raise a matter he wants to talk about.*

By the way, I see that there's still a lot of overtime being worked.
I'M GLAD YOU MENTIONED OVERTIME. I WANTED TO TAKE UP THE MATTER OF TEMPORARY STAFF.

1 temporary staff
2 Heinlein's expenses
3 Mandl's visit
4 fee for M. P. Consultants
5 agenda (for Board meeting)
6 Orpenshaw's contract
7 agreement with Passlee Electronics
8 Miss Armstrong's salary

Drill 5 *Charles Spence is attending the weekly management meeting. Downes is Chairman. Look at Spence's copy of the agenda. On it he has made notes of some small points he wants to make, and questions he wants to ask.*

AGENDA

1 Minutes of last meeting (Can we receive copies earlier?)
2 Matters arising
  i) Heinlein's expenses (I have written to him as requested)
  ii) Fee for M. P. Consultants (Has the fee been agreed?)
  iii) Temporary staff (How many are we employing?)
3 Trading account to 30 June (Does not include sales to Japan)
4 Market survey (When can we expect full report?)
5 Insurance (Our claim has been accepted by the insurance company)
6 Any other business (Can we meet an hour earlier next week?)

Now, any comments on the minutes of the last meeting, Charles?
AS FAR AS I'M CONCERNED, I'D JUST LIKE TO ASK IF WE COULD RECEIVE COPIES EARLIER?

Then there's the matter of Heinlein's expenses. You have something on this I believe, Charles?
AS FAR AS I'M CONCERNED, I'D JUST LIKE TO SAY THAT I HAVE WRITTEN TO HIM, AS REQUESTED.

ACTIVE LISTENING

Mr Birley, who works for one of London's leading merchant banks, is being interviewed about the functions of a merchant bank.

1 What kinds of problems does a merchant bank solve?

....

....

2 To what extent is a merchant bank a lending organization?

3 What sort of financial advice can a merchant bank give a company?

4 If a company wants to borrow from a merchant bank, what must it do?

5 How does the bank satisfy itself that this is the case?

6 What does the bank usually want in return for the loan?

7 Why does the bank insist on having security for the loan?

8 Why is this sort of business attractive to a merchant bank?

9 What does a merchant bank hope will happen?

10 At what stage does a merchant bank withdraw its financial support and what happens then?

11 In what ways will a merchant bank try to influence the development of a company?

12 What is the ultimate objective of the merchant bank?

ROLE SIMULATION

Statement of Problem

Paul Malone feels that sooner or later Downes or the Board of Directors will ask him exactly how he proposes to market the SC1. The product is outside Bellcrest's established field, which will mean looking for new customers in new industries, such as the industrial and commercial vehicle sectors. Bellcrest has no reputation for such devices as the SC1, and suitable advertising will therefore be necessary.

Malone feels that in order to show a profit on the SC1 at the earliest possible date, it will be necessary to launch a market campaign to promote it among as wide a range of potential customers, both at home and abroad, as can be covered.

He has therefore called together those people who could normally participate in a market campaign, with a view to working out the outlines, and the costs, of a market campaign, so that if he is asked he has a plan ready to hand. Those called to the meeting are Roger Winfield (Malone's Assistant), Dennis Evans, Charles Spence, Tom Driver, Gerald Durban (Head of Public Relations and Advertising), Tim Howatt (Sales Literature Editor), William Jenkins (Head of the Overseas Sales Department), Henry Wall (Head of Market Research) and Jean Smith (Secretary).

Re-enact this meeting and draft an outline of a market campaign to promote sales of the SC1 both in the U.K. and Europe.

Written follow-up Write up a draft of the market campaign you have decided on.

DESCRIPTION OF ROLES

Paul Malone

You called the meeting and are in the chair. You should draw up an agenda for the meeting. You should persist with the meeting until you feel you have enough of a plan for a market campaign and its costs to answer any questions Downes or the Board may put to you. Some points for you to consider are:— costs, advertising, available resources, actual and potential customers both in the U.K. and abroad, sales literature, delivery, storage space, prices, discounts for large orders and demonstrations.

Roger Winfield, Assistant to Paul Malone

You have been asked by Malone to act at the meeting as if you were the Product Executive for the SC1. If Alan Beeston joins Bellcrest, you will be required to hand over to him a coherent brief on the market campaign decided on at this meeting. You are therefore responsible for co-ordinating any plan for a market campaign, and should look at the campaign as a whole. You can call on your colleagues for background information.

Dennis Evans

You will be required to give information (which you may invent) on U.K. customers who might buy the SC1. You should also prepare a statement on how you think these customers should be approached — letter, visit of a salesman, demonstration, etc.

Charles Spence

You must ensure that the costs of the campaign do not rise too high. You should fix a budget for the campaign, which you must not allow the meeting to exceed. During the meeting you should ensure that no plans are accepted that are going to cost too much and result in overstepping the allocation of money you have fixed for the campaign.

Tom Driver

You should be prepared to say how many SC1's you can produce in a month — a figure you should invent. You should also be prepared to tell the meeting what monthly deliveries you can make, and whether you need extra storage space in the factory, or even in different parts of the country for quick distribution. You should also work out when you will be able to start producing the SC1.

Gerald Durban, Head of Public Relations and Advertising

You should be prepared to make suggestions as to what advertising media would be best to promote the SC1. Some points for you to consider are trade magazines, visits by salesmen, direct mail shots, demonstrations and samples.

Tim Howatt, Sales Literature Editor

You should be prepared to make suggestions as to what supporting literature should be prepared for the campaign. Some points for you to consider are leaflets, technical descriptions, films and slides.

William Jenkins, Head of the Overseas Sales Department
You should be prepared to report on actual and potential customers in Europe. At the meeting you are very concerned that your colleagues pay adequate attention to the European market. You feel strongly that the market campaign should be suited to European conditions, and should fight for what you want. Some points for you to consider are literature in European languages, visits by salesmen, advertisements in German, French and other languages. You want to be able to spend money in Europe on promoting the SC1.

Henry Wall, Head of Market Research
You are annoyed that Bellcrest should have called in M.P. Consultants rather than ask you to carry out a market survey on the SC1. You have spent the last week telephoning and writing to potential customers, and should be prepared to produce the results of your enquiries, which should be encouraging – these you may invent. Having found a lot of potential customers, you should say exactly how they should be approached – after all, you found them.

Jean Smith
Your job is to keep the minutes of the meeting and give a summary of the plans made at the end.

EPISODE 11 BEFORE THE BOARD

As Downes had decided not to discuss the SC1 at the last Board meeting. Malone had more time to prepare a full report on the SC1. This report had to be ready for circulation by the 20th August, and Malone started work on it immediately.

When Driver gave him the production figures for the report on the SC1, Malone at first couldn't believe them. Driver maintained that Bellcrest's production capacity would have to be increased by 20% if they were to go ahead with the SC1. Driver gave three reasons for this. Firstly, the fire had affected production, secondly Bellcrest had a lot of new, long-term orders for existing product lines, and thirdly, Orpenshaw had changed the specifications of the SC1 itself, making it a much bigger production job. Malone decided he would have to look into this in detail on the following day.

When Malone finished his report, he submitted it to Downes, who said it was simply not good enough. Malone asked him why he thought this, and Downes replied that he doubted if the Board would agree to back the SC1 on the evidence given in the report. There were the discouraging findings from M.P. Consultants, there were Tom Driver's production figures and there were Malone's own sales forecasts, which Downes felt were far too optimistic. Despite Malone's objections, Downes refused to change his opinion, although he respected Malone's enthusiasm and convictions. Malone asked if he could arrange a demonstration of the SC1 for the Board, and Downes agreed, although he doubted if Malone could arrange one in the two weeks before the Board meeting.

Malone immediately went to see Orpenshaw and asked him whether he could rig up a demonstration of the SC1 for the Board. Orpenshaw told him he was mad, as he should know it was much too early to put the SC1 in a vehicle. Malone insisted. He told Orpenshaw he would give him all the help he could, but that in two weeks the SC1 must be fitted to some sort of vehicle.

Malone then returned to his office, where he had a telephone call from Dr Perkins. Dr Perkins had some very good news from Cremorne Cars for him

Two weeks later the Board met. Malone was present to explain and defend his report. His proposal to revive the SC1 was greeted with a mixture of surprise and scepticism. Needham pointed out that the SC1 was a new product and that as 80% of all new products failed, he wondered what made the SC1 so much better than other AC speed controls. To this Malone replied that up till then speed controls of this sort had been large and heavy, whereas the SC1 was small, light and could be offered at a low price. Sir Keith Frisby, a member of the Board and an engineer, stated that what he knew of the SC1 led him to believe that Bellcrest had made an important technical breakthrough. Despite Sir Keith's support for the SC1, the Board remained unconvinced. They also wanted to know who actually used an AC speed control and what potential market there was for it. Malone drew their attention to a supplement to his report, in which full details of potential customers were given. When one Board member asked if they could see the SC1 itself, Malone invited them to a demonstration.

The Board were very impressed with the demonstration. Malone disclosed that the small electric car was being developed for city use by Cremorne Cars, who had asked Bellcrest to carry out some tests for them using the SC1 Spence was enthusiastic about the SC1, which was unusal for him, and even Needham was impressed.

When the Board returned to the Boardroom, there was quite a different atmosphere. Downes re-opened the discussion by pointing out that Ashburnham's Bank would only continue the loan if Bellcrest needed it to finance worthwhile development projects. Needham interrupted to say that in his opinion the SC1 was not a worthwhile project, and referred to the required increase of 20% in Bellcrest's production capacity. He also wanted to know where the money would come from to increase Bellcrest's production capacity. One of the Board members suggested that the money could be advanced by Ashburnham's, but Needham stated that he doubted very much whether the Bank would advance money just to launch the SC1. He went on to suggest that it might be better to sub-contract. Downes intervened to point out that sub-contracting would mean that Bellcrest would lose the chance of diversifying successfully, something that the Bank itself insisted on. Downes was supported by the other Board members, and a motion was passed stating that Bellcrest 'should continue development of the SC1 and that the Chairman should look for the necessary capital, starting with the Bank'. Needham refused to support the motion.

After the meeting Downes tried to find out from Needham why he was opposing the SC1. Needham, however, refused to tell him. He merely said he had a train to catch, that he was not in a position to comment and that the final decision was Sir Frederick's, not his. He made the mistake of telling Downes that Bellcrest was not the only firm developing an AC speed control. Downes knew that the only other firm in this field was Electrovans, and realized that Electrovans must be Bellcrest's rival for the Bank's money and that it was from Electrovans that Needham had been getting his information, and not from Janet Malone as Needham had implied at the last Board meeting. Downes was naturally furious at this.

When Malone came to see him, Downes said he owed Janet an apology. Malone was also extremely angry with Needham, and agreed with Downes that he would have to pick up some flowers on his way home! Downes promised Malone that Electrovans would not get the money from the Bank to develop their speed control if he had anything to do with it. Malone now had both the Board's and Downes' support for the SC1.

When Needham returned to the Bank, he saw Sir Frederick Ashburnham. Despite Needham's support for Electrovans, Sir Frederick stated that he had not yet made up his mind which company to support.

UNIT SUMMARY

Structures **The structures dealt with in this unit are:**

1 Reported Speech:
Present Perfect to Past Perfect:
They should *have sent* that report by now.
Well, they told me they *had sent* that report already.
Revision of tenses dealt with in Episode 8.

2 Indirect Questions :
I wonder how he knew that.
He asked me if he could attend the meeting.

3 'Could have' v. 'was able to':
He *could have* arrived already, I suppose.
He *was able to* make the necessary arrangements.

Vocabulary **The areas of vocabulary dealt with in this unit are:**

1 Looking at a report.
2 Offering advice on a proposal.
3 Putting forward a motion.

COMPREHENSION QUESTIONS

1 Why did Malone have more time to prepare his report?
2 When did this report have to be ready?
3 When did Malone start work on it?
4 Did Malone believe Driver's production figures?
5 What did Driver's figures indicate?
6 What reasons did Driver give for this?
7 What was Malone's reaction to this?
8 What did Downes think of Malone's report?
9 Why did Downes think this?
10 Why did Downes think the Board wouldn't agree to back the SC1?
11 What did Malone ask Downes' permission for?
12 Was Downes enthusiastic about having the demonstration?
13 What did Malone ask Orpenshaw?
14 How did Orpenshaw react?
15 Did Malone insist?
16 What sort of news did Dr Perkins have for Malone?
17 When did the Board meet?
18 How was the SC1 greeted?
19 What arguments did Needham use against the SC1?
20 How did Malone handle these arguments?
21 What did Sir Keith Frisby think of the SC1?
22 What else did the Board want to know about the SC1?
23 How did Malone answer this?

24 How did the Board react to the demonstration?
25 What more did Malone tell them?
26 How did Spence react to the demonstration?
27 How did Needham react to the demonstration?
28 How did Downes re-open the discussion?
29 Did Needham now think the SC1 was a suitable project?
30 What reason did he give?
31 What else did he want to know?
32 Did Needham think the Bank would advance the money?
33 What did he go on to suggest?
34 What was Downes' reaction to this suggestion?
35 Who did the Board support, Downes or Needham?
36 What motion was passed?
37 Did Needham oppose the motion?
38 What did Downes want Needham to tell him after the meeting?
39 Did Needham tell him?
40 What did Needham tell him?
41 How did Downes find out that Needham had been getting his information from Electrovans?
42 What did Downes tell Malone he should collect on his way home?
43 Why should Malone do this?
44 What did Downes promise Malone?

EXERCISES

Exercise A **Complete the following sentences:**

1 Sir Keith Frisby was impressed by the r. on the SC1. From the report he j. that Bellcrest had made an important technical b. . Needham interrupted, and Downes insisted that Malone should be allowed to e. his report and d. his recommendations. Another Board member said that the report s. the importance of electric vehicles, although no such market e. as yet.

2 After the demonstration, Needham s. to the Board that the SC1 was not a w. project. He stated that the Bank would not a. the money to launch it, and that the best a. he could give was for Bellcrest to s. -c. to a firm that was better s. to making such products.

3 One of the Board members wished to put a m. to the e. that the company should continue development of the SC1. He also suggested that the Chairman should look for the necessary c. The m. was duly s. and p. by a large majority. Needham did not s. the m. , although he was the only one to o. it.

Exercise B *Downes and Malone discussed the SC1 last week.*
Write a report of their conversation using these verbs:

For Downes: suggest, feel, enquire, believe, maintain, add, ask, wonder.
For Malone: insist, regret, disclose, complain, explain, deny, admit, assure.

Downes: Well, Paul, it's my belief that the SC1 is finished.
Malone: Really, I must protest. You're not giving me the support I need.
Downes: A question, Paul. Why is the SC1 going to be such a big production job?
Malone: There's a simple explanation. Orpenshaw has changed the specifications.
Downes: I see. And another thing: the report is taking a long time.
Malone: I have to tell you I haven't finished it.
Downes: Your wife has been rather indiscreet, hasn't she?
Malone: No, not at all. She doesn't give away company secrets.
Downes: Well, what about the consultants? Are they any good, I wonder?
Malone: Oh, don't worry. They're a very sound firm.
Downes: I have a feeling rumours really aren't enough, you know.
Malone: I'm sorry I can't get anything in writing.
Downes: And why must you make such a secret of the demonstration?
Malone: Well, I think I can tell you that Cremorne Cars have agreed to let us carry out tests with their car.
Downes: I still say there may not be any car for all we know.
Malone: Look, I'm certain about this, I tell you. Cremorne Cars are intending to develop a commuter car.

Exercise C **Complete the following sentences:**

Example:
Have you ever been to Majorca?
He asked if I had ever been to Majorca.

1 Have you seen Needham recently?
He asked

2 Is there any chance of reviving the SC1?
He wondered

3 Do you know what time the meeting is?
He asked

4 I don't understand why the Bank is withdrawing the loan.
He didn't know

5 Tell me how the SC1 works.
Spence wanted to know

6 I have my doubts about the suitability of the SC1
Needham doubted suitable.

7 Will the report be ready soon?
He asked

8 I'd like to know who takes the minutes.
He wanted to find out

9 Did we decide to sell the SC1? I can't remember.
He couldn't remember

10 Does the meeting begin at two or half past two?
He wasn't sure half past two.

Exercise D **Complete these sentences using 'could have' or 'was able to':**

Malone's first problem was production. If he had wanted to,Driver (insist) on the impossibility of producing the SC1, but Malone (persuade) him that production capacity could be increased sufficiently. Due to postponement of the discussion until the next Board meeting, Malone (spend) more time on the report but in spite of his efforts he (not convince) Downes. The Managing Director (abandon) the SC1 at this point, but Malone (get) permission to arrange a demonstration for the Board. Bad news from M.P. Consultants (also endanger) the project but fortunately Dr Perkins (produce) some encouraging figures. All this meant that Malone (put forward) a good case for the SC1. The Board agreed to support the project, although they (so easily reject) it.

Exercise E **Written Task**

At the demonstration, Sir Keith Frisby was very impressed by the performance of the SC1. As an engineer he wanted to find out as much as he could about it, so he wrote to Malone. Write this letter for him.

to congratulate you
most impressed
would like to know more
assure you of my support.

DRILLS

Drill 1 *Bellcrest has treated the SC1 as highly confidential, but it is very difficult to keep things secret in the motor industry. There have been a great many rumours. So many, in fact, that Bellcrest's competitors don't know what to believe.*

I've heard that Bellcrest have decided to expand.
ARE YOU SURE OF THAT? WHEN I LAST SPOKE TO DOWNES HE TOLD ME THAT THE RANGE OF PRODUCTS HAD BEEN REDUCED.

I believe they have spent a lot on development.
ARE YOU SURE OF THAT? WHEN I LAST SPOKE TO ORPENSHAW HE COMPLAINED THAT R. AND D. PROJECTS HAD BEEN AXED.

1 Downes/told/range of products/reduce
2 Orpenshaw/complained/R. and D. projects/axe
3 Malone/said/the project/abandon
4 Needham/told/the patents/sell

5 Driver/insisted/the offer/reject
6 Urwin/denied/a contract/sign
7 Needham/admitted/Bellcrest's proposals/consider
8 Spence/insisted/the question/not discuss

Drill 2 *The Directors of Bellcrest went to the R. and D. area to watch a demonstration of the SC1. This demonstration was also watched by Bill and Harry, two of the cleaners at the factory. They knew nothing about the SC1, and had no idea what was going on. They were interested but didn't understand what they had seen, and afterwards they had this conversation.*

Bill, who were these men?
I'VE NO IDEA WHO THEY WERE.

Bill, does that car run on batteries?
I'VE NO IDEA WHAT IT RUNS ON.

Drill 3 Did Orpenshaw make the SC1 smaller?
YES, FORTUNATELY HE WAS ABLE TO MAKE THE SC1 SMALLER.

Did he insist on having more time?
WELL, HE COULD HAVE INSISTED ON HAVING MORE TIME, BUT HE DIDN'T.

1 yes	3 well	5 yes	7 yes
2 well	4 yes	6 well	8 well

Dialogue **Showing a product to a visitor**

Paul Malone is showing one of Bellcrest's products to a visitor.

I SHOULD BE VERY HAPPY	TO GIVE YOU
I'd be glad	

ANY FURTHER INFORMATION	YOU MAY NEED ON IT.
details	require.

IF I MAY REFER YOU TO	PAGE EIGHT OF THE BROCHURE,
If I may draw your attention to	leaflet,
If you'd like to look at	

YOU'LL FIND ALL THE SPECIFICATIONS THERE.

OUR TESTS INDICATE THAT THIS MODEL HAS A SERVICE LIFE OF
show / minimum service life of
AT LEAST 55,000 HOURS.

OH, NO, FAR FROM IT.	THAT'S ABOUT	5,000 HOURS LONGER
Oh, no, not at all.	approximately	
Oh, no, certainly not.		

THAN ANY OTHER MAKE IN ITS PRICE RANGE.
all other makes at that price.

IF THAT WERE TO HAPPEN,	JUST	CONTACT
If that did happen.	you only have to	get in touch with

OUR NEAREST AGENT AND HE'LL SEND SOMEONE ROUND IMMEDIATELY.
a man
at once.
the same day.

YES, WE DO INDEED. OUR USUAL FIGURE IS AROUND 5%,
Certainly we do. trust hear

BUT THAT DEPENDS ON THE SIZE OF THE ORDER.
how large the order is.

NOT AT ALL. I HOPE WE SHALL BE HEARING FROM YOU
trust hear
VERY SHORTLY.
soon.

Drill 4 *A telephone call has just been put through to Paul Malone's office.*

Yes.
Oh, yes . . .
That's right.
Mmm . . . . .
Mm-hm . . .
That's marvellous!
Oh dear!
I'm afraid so.
No . . .
No.
That's splendid!
No, that's all right.
Fine.
Thank you very much, Mr. Veazy.
Mr. Veazy.

Drill 5 *Malone is very pleased with the car supplied by Cremorne Cars for the demonstration of the SC1. After the demonstration, he sends a telegram to Cremorne Cars. He dictates the telegram letter by letter to the telephonist.*

K. VEAZY. CREMORNE CARS SLOUGH. CONGRATULATIONS. YOUR W. J. PROTOTYPE IDEAL OUR PURPOSES. DEMONSTRATION UNQUALIFIED SUCCESS. MALONE.

ACTIVE LISTENING

Malone is ringing up Alan Beeston to offer him the post of Product Executive.

1 Why does Malone offer to wait a week for his decision?

. . . .

. . . .

2 What does Beeston want to know about his salary?

. . . .

. . . .

3 How much better off will he be in his new job?

. . . .

. . . .

4 Who are Beeston's present employers and when will he stop working for them?

. . . .

. . . .

5 Why does Malone want Beeston to start work quickly, do you think, and why can't Beeston do so?

. . . .

. . . .

6 What does Beeston want Bellcrest to help him do?

. . . .

. . . .

7 What help will Bellcrest provide?

. . . .

. . . .

8 Why will Beeston visit Bellcrest the following week?

. . . .

. . . .

9 What must he bring with him?

. . . .

. . . .

10 Why does Malone want to know Beeston's bank account number?

. . . .

. . . .

11 What does Beeston want Malone to do, and why?

. . . .

. . . .

ROLE SIMULATION

Statement of Problem

In this episode the Bellcrest Board discussed Malone's report and came to a decision on whether or not to support the SC1.

You should now re-enact this Board meeting. It is not necessary for you to come to the same decision as the Board did. Use your own judgement. Malone, the Marketing Manager, has submitted his report to you, and you are free to ask him any further questions you like before coming to a decision. The demonstration has already taken place.

Written follow-up

Write a summary of your discussion and the decision you reached.

DESCRIPTION OF ROLES

Maurice Downes

You are in the chair at the meeting. It is up to you to guide the discussion and to see that everyone present can have his say. You are prepared to help Malone defend his report if necessary.

Paul Malone

It is up to you to convince the Board that the SC1 would be a worthwhile project. You have given the members your report, and have given them a demonstration. Your report contains not only Driver's production figures (production capacity must be raised by 20%) and M.P. Consultants' findings but also a supplementary report on potential customers, in which you have mentioned Cremorne Cars and D.A.U. You are free to invent further potential customers if necessary. You should prepare your arguments in favour of the SC1 carefully and at the meeting be ready to fight for your project.

Edward Needham

You are determined to stop the SC1 if possible. You will do everything you can to make Bellcrest realize that the Bank will not advance the money which you consider is required for this project. Remember the possibility of persuading Bellcrest to sub-contract to another company. You should prepare as many arguments as you can against the SC1.

Charles Spence

You have been impressed by Malone's demonstration, but are still ready to be convinced either way. You hate Needham.

Miss Armstrong

Your job is to keep the minutes of the meeting, and to give a summary of the discussion and decisions reached at the end.

Sir Keith Frisby

You are an engineer. You know the SC1 is technically brilliant and that Bellcrest has made an important technical breakthrough. You are not, however, convinced that Bellcrest is the right company to develop it and are worried about withdrawal of the Bank loan.

David March

Your first reaction was against the SC1, but you were impressed by the demonstration. You now have an open mind, but want more information before you finally decide one way or the other.

Angus Hamilton

Your first reaction was against the SC1, but you were impressed by the demonstration. You now have an open mind, but want more information before you finally decide one way or the other.

Alderman Jackson

Your first reaction was against the SC1, but you were impressed by the demonstration. You now have an open mind, but want more information before you finally decide one way or the other.

William Forbes

Your first reaction was against the SC1, and you were not impressed by the demonstration. You are in complete agreement with Needham, and think that the risk of entering the automotive field is too great for Bellcrest to take. You think the Bank is not likely to finance the project. You have severe indigestion and are in a bad temper.

EPISODE 12 APPOINTMENTS

Downes now had the approval of his Board to go ahead with the SC1 provided that Bellcrest could raise the necessary capital. He had also learned that Electrovans were competing for the Bank's money to develop their own AC speed control, and that Needham at least was backing them, so the obvious source for the money Bellcrest needed was very uncertain. Downes decided to ring up Sir Frederick so as to arrange a meeting.

Sir Frederick was pleased to have some definite information about Bellcrest's plans so that he could assess their claim to the Bank's money. Sir Frederick had already discussed Bellcrest's last Board meeting with Needham, from which he understood that Bellcrest wanted the money so as to finance the launching of the SC1. Downes asked for a meeting so that he could explain how the SC1 would benefit the Bank, and added that he did not feel Bellcrest was being fairly represented by Needham. Sir Frederick agreed to a discussion, but said he would not be free until the following week.

Soon after Downes had finished speaking to Sir Frederick, he had a telephone call from Sam Urwin in Toronto. Urwin wanted to meet Downes to discuss something that he described as being personal and urgent. Downes would have preferred to meet Urwin after talking to Sir Frederick the following Wednesday, but Urwin insisted on meeting him before then as he was visiting Electrovans on Wednesday and he had to make an important decision before seeing Williams. Downes agreed to see him the following Tuesday.

Urwin arrived the following Tuesday. As he was walking to Bellcrest he was almost run over by one of the Cremorne electric cars. Downes, who was watching from his window, was amused by this, but felt he had better get Driver to issue a memo to all drivers telling them to be more careful in future.

When Urwin arrived in Downes' office he said he wanted to talk about Donald Williams and Electrovans in the strictest confidence. He asked for Downes' advice on whether he could trust Williams, and showed Downes a brochure that Electrovans had recently distributed in North America which implied that his corporation was already an Electrovans customer, which was not in fact the case. Urwin said it was true that he was negotiating

with Williams, and that negotiations had reached the stage where he had to say 'yes' or 'no'. He added that although a contract had been drafted it had not yet been signed. Urwin had looked at Electrovans' company records and said they looked all right, but he still wasn't entirely happy. Downes said that in his opinion Urwin would be safe if he signed the contract.

Downes then had a number of questions he wanted to ask Urwin. He wanted to know why Urwin had been talking to him as if he was no more than an old friend, when Bellcrest already had an agreement with Passlee Electronics. Urwin pointed out that this was a non-exclusive agreement, but Downes refused to accept this as an excuse. He accused Urwin of going behind his back, as Urwin must have known from Electrovans' sales literature that they were moving into Bellcrest's field. Urwin defended himself by saying that what he wanted was outside Bellcrest's field – an AC speed control for electric vehicles. Downes reminded Urwin of the car that had nearly run him over earlier and told him it was fitted with a Bellcrest AC speed control.

Urwin was extremely annoyed that he hadn't been told earlier that Bellcrest was developing an AC speed control. He said that if he had been kept in the picture there would have been no trouble with Electrovans, as if he had known what Bellcrest was doing he would never have gone to Electrovans at all. He said that this time Downes would regret his usual caution, but he agreed to have a look at the SC1.

After he had obtained the approval of the Board for the SC1, Malone got in touch with Alan Beeston and offered him a job as a product executive, which he accepted. When he came to Bellcrest, Malone told him he hoped he would be responsible for the SC1, though this was not yet definite. To Malone's surprise, Beeston already knew that Electrovans was developing a speed control and he had in fact turned down a job with them. He went on to say that Electrovans' future didn't look too bright, so he was glad he had not accepted it. He then revealed that Beamish Motors, who accounted for over 40% of all Electrovans' business, had stopped doing business with them and that all orders had been switched to other suppliers. Malone was astonished and hurried off to tell Downes the news.

Malone found Downes with Orpenshaw and Urwin in the Research and Development Area, where they were looking at the SC1. Orpenshaw was just telling Urwin that Electrovans was more than five years behind Bellcrest in the development of its speed control, so he was wasting his time buying from them. Urwin was clearly annoyed and obviously had plenty to say about the SC1, but said he would prefer to say it in Downes' office. Downes and Urwin then left, so Malone was unable to tell Downes the vital piece of information that Beeston had brought.

After Downes and Urwin had left, Orpenshaw said he was surprised that nobody had told Urwin about the SC1. Malone agreed that this time Downes' caution had lost the biggest customer they were likely to get.

UNIT SUMMARY

Structures The structures dealt with in this unit are:

1 Conditionals:

a If you *phoned* Orpenshaw I'm sure he *would tell* you.

b If Urwin *had known* about the SC1 *he would not have approached* Electrovans.

2 Connectives: 'so', 'so that', and 'so as to'.

a The report was not ready, *so* the meeting was postponed.

b Bellcrest wanted the Bank's money *so that* they could develop the SC1.

c We needed information *so as to* assess your claim.

3 Telegrams:

The composition and understanding of telegrams.

Vocabulary The areas of vocabulary dealt with in this unit are:

1 Approval/source/back.

2 Assess/claim.

3 Appointments.

dditional notes **Exercise C**

A common mistake is the use of 'so that' instead of 'so'. This exercise therefore concentrates on the use of 'so' as a connective although there are one or two examples of 'so that' and 'so as to'. In examples 1 and 9, encourage the students to use 'so as to' plus infinitive rather than 'so that' plus 'can' or 'will'. Notice that in colloquial English the word 'that' is often omitted from the connective 'so that'.

COMPREHENSION QUESTIONS

1 On what condition could Downes go ahead with the SC1?
2 What had he found out about Electrovans?
3 Why did Electrovans want the Bank's money?
4 Why was it uncertain that Bellcrest would get the Bank's money?
5 Why did Downes ring up Sir Frederick?
6 Why was Sir Frederick pleased to have some definite information?
7 Why did Sir Frederick think Bellcrest wanted the money?
8 Why did Downes ask for a meeting?
9 When would Sir Frederick be free?
10 Why did Urwin want to see Downes?
11 When did Downes want to see Urwin?
12 Why did Urwin insist on meeting Downes on Tuesday?
13 What did Urwin have to do before going to Electrovans?
14 What happened to Urwin on his way to Downes' office?
15 What memo did Driver issue?
16 Did Urwin want anyone else to hear his discussion with Downes?
17 What advice did Urwin want?
18 What worried Urwin about the brochure he showed Downes?

19 Was Urwin an Electrovans customer?
20 At what stage in his negotiations was Urwin?
21 Had the contract been signed?
22 What advice did Downes give Urwin?
23 What did Downes want to know from Urwin?
24 What sort of agreement did Bellcrest have with Passlee Electronics?
25 Why did Downes accuse Urwin of being underhand?
26 How did Urwin defend himself?
27 What was Urwin's reaction when Downes told him that Bellcrest had an AC speed control?
28 Would Urwin have turned to Electrovans if he had known about the SC1?
29 What job did Malone offer Beeston?
30 Would Beeston be responsible for the SC1?
31 Why was Beeston glad he hadn't accepted a job with Electrovans?
32 Why is Electrovans' future not too bright?
33 What was Malone's reaction to this news?
34 What were Downes and Urwin doing in the R. and D. area?
35 Why did Orpenshaw tell Urwin he was wasting his time with Electrovans?
36 Did Malone tell Downes Beeston's news?
37 What did Malone think the reason would be if they lost Urwin as a customer?

EXERCISES

Exercise A **Complete the following sentences:**

1 At the Board meeting Downes won the a. of his Board to g. a. with the SC1 provided that he could r. the money to l. it. Ashburnham's Bank, the obvious s. of this money, seemed to be b. Electrovans so Downes rang Sir Frederick to arrange a meeting to discuss the whole matter.

2 Sir Frederick was glad to have the information on the SC1, as he could then a. Bellcrest's c. to the Bank's money. Downes told Sir Frederick he could argue Bellcrest's c. in detail against any r. the Bank could p. u.

3 Sir Frederick told his secretary to a. an a. with Downes for the following week. His secretary wanted to know what time would s. Downes, who told her that three o'clock on Wednesday would be c.

Exercise B **Complete the following sentences:**

Urwin: Maurice, I almost got run down in the yard just now. I was walking over to the main office when this damn little car nearly took the pants off me. If he (blow) his horn, I (hear) him and gotten out of the way.

Downes: My apologies, Sam. But if you (look) where you were going, you (see) him, I expect.

Urwin: Well, if your drivers (race) around like that every day as they seem to be doing, you (soon have) some

	accidents. Maybe if you (tell) them to be careful, do you think they (drive) a little slower?
Downes:	Yes, if we (tell) our drivers to drive slowly, then they (do) it.
Urwin:	If you (can) do that, I (be) grateful.
Downes:	We don't have accidents here, you know.
Urwin:	If you (do have) an accident, it (really wake you up) wouldn't it?
Downes:	O.K. I (ask) Driver to see to it if you (think) it's necessary.
Urwin:	Thanks. Then if I (go out) again, maybe I (not get) run over. And if you (do) that before, I (not be) in danger in the first place.

Exercise C

When Malone writes down notes in his diary he often uses signs instead of words so as to save time.

For example he uses the sign → to show either *the reason for* or *the result of* an action.

Example:
Give Downes the facts → he can present his report.
I'll have to give Downes the facts so that he can present his report.

Here are some notes from Malone's diary.
Make complete sentences using: 'so/so that/so as to'.

1 Present a strong case → be able to convince the Board.
2 Get hold of car → have to negotiate with Cremorne Cars.
3 Orpenshaw arrange demonstration → Board will see the advantages.
4 Brief Beeston → Jean will have to make an appointment for next week.
5 Must see Urwin → must find out which hotel he's in.
6 Forget to give Driver report → figures have not been checked.
7 Write to Mandl → answer his questions.
8 Jean off sick → Betty must type letters.
9 Take car into garage → engine can be repaired.
10 Downes says Janet indiscreet → must ask her about Needham.

Exercise D

You have received the following telegrams.
Write out the messages in complete sentences.

1 SEND SIX HUNDRED OFF FIVE TWO SEVENS STOP
2 MEET REP ARRIVING PANAM FOUR THREE ONE WEDNESDAY STOP
3 PRESIDENT PASSLEE QUOTE DEAL OFF UNQUOTE STOP ARRANGE MEETING STOP

4 NEED SURGE DIVERTERS URGENT STOP ORDER FIVE HUNDRED STOP
5 ORDER EIGHTH INST UNARRIVED STOP ATTEND URGENT STOP

Exercise E **Written Task**

Malone has to write to Beeston confirming an offer he made by telephone. You write this letter for him. Use these notes:

Offer you post of Product Executive
Start September 14th
Salary £2,500
4 weeks holiday
Duties
Assistance with accommodation
Please confirm acceptance
Send insurance card, bank account number

DRILLS

Drill 1 Bellcrest wants to diversify.
THEY WOULD DIVERSIFY IF THEY LAUNCHED A NEW PRODUCT.

1 launch/new product
2 Bank/approve/project
3 facts/figures/ready
4 know/project
5 demonstrate/SC1

Williams left Bellcrest
HE WOULDN'T HAVE LEFT IF DOWNES HADN'T GIVEN HIM THE SACK.

6 Downes/give/sack
7 Williams/copy/design
8 Bank/threaten/withdraw loan
9 Downes/keep/in the dark
10 Malone/warn

Drill 2 Why did Bellcrest have to ask for a loan?
THEY HAD TO ASK FOR A LOAN SO AS TO FINANCE NEW PROJECTS.

And why were all those new projects launched?
THEY WERE LAUNCHED SO THAT LONG-TERM PROFITS COULD BE INCREASED.

1 finance new projects
2 long-term profits/can/be increased
3 capture a growing market
4 meeting/can/arrange
5 obtain the facts
6 Bank/can/assess/Bellcrest's claim
7 financial questions/can/settle
8 avoid/see/Needham

Dialogue **Arranging a meeting**

Sam Urwin telephones Downes to arrange a meeting for the following week.

SAM! WHERE ARE YOU SPEAKING FROM?
phoning
calling

TOWARDS THE END OF THE WEEK WOULD SUIT ME BEST.
be best for me.
be most convenient for me.

I'LL BE IN LONDON ON WEDNESDAY. WOULD THAT BE ANY USE TO YOU
Would that help you at all?

SORRY, SAM. THIS LINE'S BAD. WOULD YOU MIND REPEATING THA
awful. Would you say that again?
terrible.

WOULD TUESDAY AFTERNOON BE ALL RIGHT?
suit you?

I CAN'T MANAGE THE MORNING.
I can't make the morning.
I'm tied up in the morning.

YES, OF COURSE, SAM, WHAT'S ALL THE HURRY ABOUT?
why the hurry?

I SEE. WELL, I LOOK FORWARD TO SEEING
Ah ha. meeting
YOU ON TUESDAY AFTERNOON. TWO THIRTY'D BE FINE.
quite all right.

BYE, SAM.
Cheerio, Sam.

Drill 3 *Alan Beeston is in Paul Malone's office. They are discussing Beeston's new job. Beeston has a number of things for which he wants to ask Malone's permission.*

I'm hoping Bellcrest will pay my removal expenses. I don't think it'll be very much.
I'M SURE THAT'LL BE ALL RIGHT, AS LONG AS IT ISN'T TOO MUCH.

Drill 4 *Beeston and Malone are still talking. Malone is telling Beeston about his work at Bellcrest. Beeston has a number of questions he wants to ask.*

Now, you'll be doing several kinds of work.
BEFORE WE GO ANY FURTHER, I'D LIKE TO KNOW SOMETHING MORE ABOUT THE KINDS OF WORK I'LL BE DOING.

ACTIVE LISTENING

Malone thinks that the AC speed control developed by Electrovans will infringe Bellcrest's patents. He decided to consult Mr Howard, a specialist in patent law.

1 Who suggested that Malone should consult Howard?

2 What does Malone do first before discussing his problem with Howard?

3 When he has heard this, what is the first thing Howard wants to know?

4 What has led Malone to suspect that there has been an infringement of patents?

5 What did Orpenshaw think he would have to do if he joined the other firm?

6 Why does Howard advise Malone to get more information?

7 At what point does an infringement of patent occur?

8 Why is it difficult for Malone to confirm his suspicions?

9 In what way is British patent law different from that of many other European countries?

10 Could Malone go to a law court at this stage?

11 What does Howard warn Malone about?

12 What does he advise him to do?

Statement of Problem Alan Beeston will be taking up his appointment at the beginning of next week. During his first week with Bellcrest he will need to be introduced to the work of a number of departments. It has therefore been suggested that he should meet the Heads of the Departments with whom he will have to co-operate. Malone's secretary, Jean Smith, has tried to draw up a timetable for Beeston's first week, but unfortunately everybody's diaries are rather full.

Beeston himself wants to visit the various departments in a particular order. As Malone wants the timetable settled as quickly as possible, he has asked all those concerned to drop into his office at 5.30, after work, to be introduced to Beeston and arrange a time when he can call on them the following week.

The object of this short meeting is therefore to arrange a timetable for Beeston without interfering with anyone's existing arrangements.

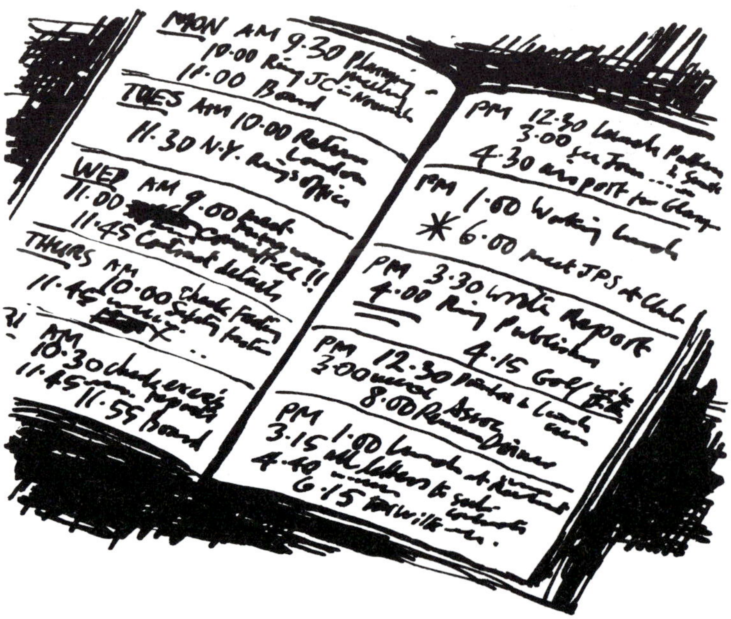

Written follow-up Imagine you are Jean Smith. Draw up a timetable for Beeston as decided on at your meeting, stating the purpose of each meeting that has been arranged.

DESCRIPTION OF ROLES

Paul Malone

You must get Beeston's timetable settled. You should know why you want Beeston to visit these people. Your own diary reads as follows.

Monday	10.00	See Downes	Thursday	D.A.U.
	12.30	Lunch with Urwin		
Tuesday	9.30	Management meeting	Friday	D.A.U.
Wednesday	10.30	Fly to D.A.U., Germany Return Sunday		

Alan Beeston

You would prefer to visit the various departments in the following order:

1) Paul Malone. 2) Dennis Evans – Sales. 3) Bob Orpenshaw – Research and Development. 4) Tom Driver – Production. 5) Charles Spence – Company Secretary. 6) Maurice Downes. 7) David Smithson – Personnel. 8) Henry Wall – Market Research. You should work out your reasons for wanting to visit in this order and what you want to see them about. You will be handling the SC1.

Jean Smith

Your job is to make a note of each arrangement, and to tell everyone Beeston's complete timetable when this has been worked out.

Dennis Evans

You don't want to see Beeston at all. Your diary for the week in question is as follows:

Monday		Visits to customers
Tuesday	9.30	Management meeting
Wednesday	9.30	W.T.Representative
	11.00	Sales Conference
	2.00	London
Thursday		Your holidays start.

Tom Driver

You're going to be very busy this week. Here is your diary:

Monday	9.30	Meet foremen	Thursday	
	11.00	See Downes	Friday	Costings for SC1 due.
	3.00	See Malone		
Tuesday		London		
Wednesday	12.30	Lunch with Jenkinson		

Bob Orpenshaw

You have no engagements next week, but you have a lot of work to do on testing the SC1. You hate visitors at any time, and are very unco-operative.

Miss Armstrong

You are at the meeting to arrange a time for Beeston to see Mr Downes. Mr Downes is only free on Wednesday morning.

Charles Spence

You have a very busy week. The auditors are coming on Wednesday at 9 a.m., and you have to have all the accounts ready by then. You don't see the point of meeting Beeston.

Henry Wall

You want to see Beeston as soon as possible on Monday morning. You will be away from your office from 3 p.m. on Monday until the end of the week.

David Smithson

You want to see Beeston as soon as possible to arrange such things as his insurance card, and to get necessary information from him, such as his bank account number.

AGREEMENT.

Malone was unable to give Downes Beeston's information about Electrovans losing their largest customer when Downes and Urwin were in the Research and Development area, so he followed them to Downes' office. Although Downes tried to stop him, Malone insisted on attacking Urwin's decision to make a deal with Electrovans. He forced Urwin to admit that the SC1 was better than Electrovans' speed control, but Urwin immediately pointed out that Electrovans were tooled up to produce their speed control and that Williams had already given him a firm delivery date for the first units. Malone then revealed that Electrovans had just lost their biggest customer.

Downes and Urwin reacted to this news in different ways. Downes was surprised and suggested that Electrovans might be in real trouble, whereas Urwin felt this would help him as Electrovans would be freer to concentrate on producing their speed control. Malone jumped on this and said it might well not be Electrovans' speed control at all, as he was pretty sure that their design infringed the Bellcrest patents. If that was the case, he added, Bellcrest would certainly take out an injunction ordering Electrovans to stop production.

Urwin was by now very angry, as he felt that Malone and Downes were being obstructive. He said he might well cancel his agreements with Bellcrest if Bellcrest took out an injunction against Electrovans to stop production of the speed controls he urgently needed. Downes said if Urwin signed a contract with Electrovans, he would terminate the agreement himself. He went on to say that naturally he didn't expect Urwin to make a decision on trust, and Malone added that he would give Urwin all the data he needed on the SC1. Finally Urwin agreed to tell his Technical Manager to join him at Bellcrest that day rather than the following day at Electrovans, but that was as far as he would go. Urwin's decision was vital to Bellcrest.

The following day Downes went to the Bank to argue his case for the SC1, and to keep hold of the Bank's investment in Bellcrest. Before he arrived, Needham argued in favour of giving the loan to Electrovans, as he felt that they were more qualified to produce an AC speed control. Sir Frederick insisted, however, on allowing Downes to argue his case. At that moment Downes arrived with a visitor Needham was unable to identify.

Downes started his argument for the Bank's loan staying with Bellcrest by telling Sir Frederick that Electrovans had just lost all their orders from Beamish Motors, which amounted to 45% in volume of business. Needham said that this might well mean that Electrovans could concentrate on producing their speed control, and added that they already had one large and urgent order from North America. Downes then sprang a surprise on Sir Frederick and Needham by telling them that this was Passlee Electronics, and that Passlee's Executive Vice-President, Sam Urwin, was waiting outside. He asked Sir Frederick if he might invite Urwin to join them and Sir Frederick agreed, although he thought it highly irregular.

When Urwin had been introduced, he announced that he was calling off his deal with Electrovans, as the Electrovans' design appeared to infringe the Bellcrest patents. Needham said that Williams had assured him there was no infringement of the Bellcrest patents, but on Sir Frederick's asking whether the information had been checked, he had to admit that it hadn't. Needham went on to say that in any case he could see a solution to the problem, but Downes immediately interrupted him to say that Bellcrest were not going to sell the patents. Sir Frederick then asked Downes for his solution. Downes said that the Bank loan could stay with Bellcrest as the money would certainly be needed to finish development and start production of the SC1. Sir Frederick wondered how Bellcrest was going to meet orders that were needed quickly, such as Urwin's, and how and where the SC1 was actually going to be produced. Downes said that Bellcrest could sub-contract. Sir Frederick thanked him for this suggestion and announced that the loan would stay with Bellcrest, provided that Electrovans was the sub-contractor. Downes protested that he would not sit at the same table with Williams, but Sir Frederick ignored this and instructed Needham to arrange a meeting. Needham tried to prevent this, but Sir Frederick firmly said he would talk to him later.

The meeting between Downes and Williams was arranged to take place in a quiet hotel where there would be no publicity. Downes, Spence and Malone arrived first. Downes was surprised to find Joy Banks there, the journalist who had interviewed him at the time of the Bellcrest fire. When Williams arrived, he was sarcastic about Malone's presence, and told Downes that talking about the SC1 reminded him of his time at Bellcrest. He then insisted that Downes should shake hands with him, and as they did so, Joy Banks took a photograph, which appeared next day in the Midland News.

Downes was furious at this trick, and went to the Bank the following day. He asked Sir Frederick whether he realized that Williams had arranged for the photograph to be taken, and pointed out that no-one could conduct business with a man who behaved like that. Sir Frederick agreed that the incident was most unfortunate, but maintained that Electrovans were the ideal firm to make the SC1. Downes didn't deny this, but said that Williams had to go, otherwise he could not agree to Electrovans being the sub-contractor. Sir Frederick said that the Bank did not sack Managing Directors, but when Downes replied that Bellcrest should be represented on the Electrovans Board, he said the Bank would welcome such a link. Downes was immediately worried that this representative would be Needham, but Sir Frederick assured him it wouldn't. He added that Needham would be replaced as the Bank's representative on the Bellcrest Board. Sir Frederick then mentioned that Williams had been offered another job, which meant that the post of Managing Director of Electrovans would be vacant for someone Downes could trust as he was sure Williams would be wise enough to accept the job he had been offered.

Later that day Downes called on Malone and told him that he would be appointed Managing Director of Electrovans.

UNIT SUMMARY

Structures **The structures dealt with in this unit are:**

1 'Can' contrasted with 'May':
Electrocans *can* produce the SC1.
Bellcrest *may* sell the patents.

2 Modal verbs and past time reference:
He *may arrive* any minute now.
He *may have arrived* already.
He *should come* soon.
He *should have* come by now.

3 Connectives: Despite the fact that/whereas/otherwise/provided that
Downes had to agree to sub-contract to Electrovans, *despite the fact that* he hated Williams.
Downes wanted to keep the Bank's money, *whereas* Needham wanted it to go to Electrovans.
Downes said Williams must resign, *otherwise* he would.
Bellcrest could produce the SC1, *provided that* they could raise the money.

Vocabulary **The areas of vocabulary dealt with in this unit are:**

1 Trust and Confidence
2 Merger/take over.

dditional Notes **Role Simulation**

This role simulation will require a Faction Meeting (See Introductory Notes)

COMPREHENSION QUESTIONS

1 Why did Malone follow Downes and Urwin?
2 What did Malone attack?
3 What did he make Urwin admit?
4 What advantages in ordering from Electrovans were there for Urwin?
5 What news did Malone have for Urwin and Downes?
6 How did Downes and Urwin react?
7 Why didn't Malone think Electrovans' design was their own?
8 What would Bellcrest do if Electrovans had infringed their patents?
9 Why was Urwin angry?
10 What would Urwin do if Bellcrest took out an injunction?
11 In what circumstances would Downes cancel his agreement with Urwin?
12 What did Urwin agree to do?
13 How important was Urwin's decision to Bellcrest?
14 Why did Downes go to the Bank?
15 Why did Needham want the loan to go to Electrovans?
16 How did Downes open his argument?
17 How did Needham interpret the loss of Beamish Motors' business?
18 How did Downes surprise Sir Frederick and Needham?
19 Did Sir Frederick think Downes' request was a normal one?
20 Why was Urwin going to cancel his deal with Electrovans?

21 Had Needham made sure there was no infringement of Bellcrest's patents?
22 Was Downes willing to sell the patents?
23 What solution did Downes propose?
24 What point did Sir Frederick raise?
25 How did Downes react?
26 On what condition could Bellcrest keep the loan?
27 Was Downes happy about this condition?
28 Why not?
29 Who was to arrange the meeting?
30 Why was the meeting in a quiet hotel?
31 Who was Joy Banks?
32 What had Williams arranged?
33 What action did Downes take over this?
34 Did Downes think Electrovans was a suitable firm to make the SC1?
35 What link between the two companies did Sir Frederick and Downes agree on?
36 Was Needham going to continue on the Bellcrest board?
37 Why would the post of Managing Director of Electrovans soon be vacant?
38 Who was to be the new.Managing Director?

EXERCISES

Exercise A **Complete the following sentences:**

1 Downes was unwilling to co-operate with Williams mainly because he had no t.   in him. He was unable to t.   a man who had clearly been less then h.   in his dealings with Passlee Electronics. The events of five years previously had already destroyed any g.   that might have existed between the two men and left an atmosphere of m.   Downes h.   no c.   in the h.   of Williams, so when he announced that Electrovans' speed control did not infringe Bellcrest patents, Downes certainly did not t.   this on t.   and began to make enquiries about the matter. His lack of confidence in their honesty was in the end well j.   , and Downes was glad he had p.   his t.   in his own judgement.

2 Downes was anxious that Electrovans should be m.   with Bellcrest rather than becoming a c.   in the same field. Sir Frederick Ashburnham, however, was against a m.   and preferred Electrovans to manufacture the speed control units as s.   – c.   to Bellcrest. Downes opposed any such arrangement and continued to put the case for a t.   o.   . He finally agreed to Sir Frederick's proposals on condition that Bellcrest should be r.   on the Board of Electrovans by a completely t.   person.

Exercise B **Rewrite the following sentences using 'can' or 'may':**

Examples:
It's possible Williams will join Beamish Motors.
Williams may join Beamish Motors.

At last we have enough time to visit customers.
At last we can visit customers.

1 Joy Banks has a good story to write about Downes and Williams.
2 Malone will probably reorganize Electrovans.
3 He's in a position to realize all his plans.
4 The Malones are thinking about moving house.
5 Orpenshaw has the time to concentrate on his technical work now.
6 Now the Malones have enough money to buy a new car.
7 The immediate appointment of a new marketing manager is likely.
8 Downes feels able to speak to Electrovans' Managing Director now.
9 Beamish Motors will perhaps buy from Electrovans again.
10 The R. and D. section will probably be rehoused.

Exercise C *Downes, Urwin and Malone are having an argument about Urwin's deal with Electrovans.*

Complete the sentences:

Downes: If you buy from Electrovans, Sam, our agreement with Passlee may (terminate)

Urwin: Now, don't blame me for going to Electrovans. It's your own fault, Maurice. I should (tell) about the SC1 long ago.

Downes: But surely you see that it was necessary to keep it a secret? If our competitors had found out, it would (be) bad for business.

Urwin: Keeping quiet about it has been even worse for business. This deal with Electrovans might never (consider) if you had trusted me with your secret. As it is I cannot (expect) to reverse my decision now.

Malone: But, Sam, the SC1 is so much better than anything that could (design) by Electrovans.

Urwin: The Electrovans design may not (be) better than the SC1, but at least they have the resources to put it on the market. You can't deny, Paul, that the SC1 cannot (produce) without difficulty. And I just do not believe that their design infringes your patents. That must (check) before they went ahead.

Malone: You don't know Williams. Anyway, Electrovans has just lost its biggest customer. Their ability to produce could (affect) by this.

Urwin: If I had had this information earlier, I might (prepare) to cancel negotiations. But it is too late now. The contract should (sign) the day after tomorrow.

Exercise D **Complete the sentences using 'despite the fact that' and 'whereas':**

1 Urwin was negotiating a deal with Electrovans he still had an agreement with Bellcrest.
2 Williams knew about the SC1 Urwin hadn't been told.
3 Urwin wanted to buy the Electrovans speed control Bellcrest could produce a better one.
4 Downes was pessimistic about Bellcrest's chances Malone was rather more hopeful.
5 Electrovans was going ahead with its speed control it probably infringed Bellcrest patents.
6 Bellcrest intended to produce the SC1 it was right outside their normal field.
7 Electrovans was ready to produce a speed control Bellcrest had only just decided to revive their project.
8 Bellcrest was in a strong position Electrovans had just lost its biggest customer.
9 Downes is a sound man Williams is very adventurous.
10 Downes agreed to launch the new project he is usually very cautious.

Exercise E **Written Task**

Write Sir Frederick's letter to Downes confirming the extension of the loan, arrangements for production of the SC1 and management changes at Electrovans.

DRILLS

Drill 1 Is it possible that the Electrovans design infringes our patents?
YES, IT MAY INFRINGE OUR PATENTS.

If this is the case, have we the right to take legal action?
YES, WE CAN TAKE LEGAL ACTION.

Drill 2 *It is quarter to eleven and Beeston hasn't yet arrived at Bellcrest where he has an appointment for ten o'clock. Malone asks Jean about this.*

Wasn't Beeston's train due some time ago?
MM. IT SHOULD HAVE BEEN IN AN HOUR AGO.

We can expect him any time now.
MM. HE SHOULD BE HERE ANY TIME NOW.

1 should/in/an hour ago
2 should/here/any time now
3 may/coming/car
4 may/caught/rush hour
5 could/delayed/by the fog
6 might not/here/before twelve
7 must/on his way then
8 should/informed/delay
9 must/prevented/getting here
10 could/in an accident

Dialogue **Dealing with a complaint**

Paul Malone is in his office when a customer rings him up.

MALONE.
Malone here.

SPEAKING.
Yes, that's right.

I'M SORRY TO HEAR THAT, MR BURTON.
you say so,

NATURALLY NOT, MR BURTON. COULD YOU GIVE ME THE INVOICE
Of course not, NUMBER?

RIGHT, I'VE GOT THAT. I'LL LOOK INTO IT IMMEDIATELY, MR BURTON.
I see. I'll make enquiries immediately,

I'LL FIND OUT WHAT'S HAPPENED AND RING YOU BACK WITHIN HALF
I'll see phone AN HOUR.
call

OF COURSE. I'M VERY SORRY THERE'S BEEN A DELAY.
Naturally. about this delay.
I must apologize for this delay.

YOU'LL CERTAINLY HAVE THEM BY THEN, MR BURTON.
definitely receive

YES, OF COURSE.
Yes, certainly.

GOODBYE, MR BURTON.

Drill 3 *Maurice Downes and Sam Urwin are arguing about the SC1. Downes is trying to persuade Urwin to change his mind about buying from Electrovans, but Urwin is being very firm.*

I know you came to England with plans to buy the speed control, but isn't it possible to put off your decision?
LOOK HERE MAURICE, I'VE MADE UP MY MIND TO BUY THE SPEED CONTROL. I DON'T INTEND TO PUT OFF MY DECISION WITHOUT A GOOD REASON.

Drill 4 *Paul Malone has just taken up his new job as Managing Director of Electrovans. He is talking to his Marketing Manager, George Turpin. They are planning the production and marketing of the SC1.*

1 Get ready for production: complete tests/equip a production line.
2 Produce SC1: increase production capacity/find more capital.
3 Increase production capacity: work overtime/take on new staff.
4 Take on new staff: select them carefully/train them.
5 Launch the SC1: prepare brochures/plan publicity campaign.
6 Sell the SC1: find customers/appoint agents.
7 Export the SC1: appoint overseas agents/learn foreign languages.
8 Learn a foreign language: attend a course/work hard.

ACTIVE LISTENING

Malone makes the acquaintance of Mr MacLeod, the Managing Director of a subsidiary company, and invites him home to discuss the problems of subsidiaries. Their wives can be heard talking in the background.

1 Has Mr MacLeod's company always been a subsidiary?

. . . .

. . . .

2 Why did the parent company take over a number of smaller firms?

. . . .

. . . .

3 What types of companies were taken over?

. . . .

. . . .

4 Why was Mr MacLeod's company included in the group?

. . . .

. . . .

5 What differences are there between being the Managing Director of an independent company and the Managing Director of a subsidiary?

. . . .

. . . .

6 Are there any disadvantages in being the Managing Director of a subsidiary?

. . . .

. . . .

7 What does the parent company try to persuade subsidiaries to do?

. . . .

. . . .

8 What directorships does Mr MacLeod hold?

. . . .

. . . .

9 What does he mean when he says there is a 'conflict of loyalty' in this set-up?

. . . .

. . . .

10 Why is this combine not typical of British combines?

. . . .

. . . .

11 In what way is this subsidiary company in a special position within the group?

. . . .

. . . .

12 What effect has this had on the parent group?

. . . .

ROLE SIMULATION

Statement of Problem

Sir Frederick has decided to call a meeting at which all parties concerned with the Bank's loan are to represented. The purpose of the meeting is to decide whether the Bank's money is to be invested in Bellcrest or Electrovans, or whether a compromise solution should be found. A number of suggestions for a compromise have been made. They include the suggestion that there should be a merger between the two companies, that Bellcrest should sub-contract to Electrovans, and that Bellcrest should sell the SC1 patents to Electrovans and give up this particular field of activity.

Re-enact this meeting and come to your own solution. It is not necessary that you should come to the same solution as Sir Frederick did in the film. What is your solution?

Written follow-up Write a summary of the agreement you have reached.

DESCRIPTION OF ROLES

The Bank

Sir Frederick Ashburnham

You are impartial. You are concerned to arrive at the most satisfactory solution from the Bank's point of view. The sum you want to invest in the electronics industry is £300,000, and you want an arrangement that will show the most profitable return on your investment. You are in the chair at the meeting. You will have to announce your decision at the end. You must come to a solution, and can use the loan as a stick to beat the others into agreement with you if this turns out to be necessary.

Edward Needham

You very much want Electrovans to have the Bank's money, and should prepare arguments to support them. Remember that Electrovans is tooled up to produce a speed control, whereas Bellcrest are not. Furthermore, Electrovans is more suited to the production of a device like the SC1 than Bellcrest. You should also think of a solution profitable to Electrovans.

Secretary

Your job is to keep the minutes of the meeting. You are a little deaf, and so have to interrupt frequently to have things repeated.

Bellcrest

Maurice Downes

You want to keep the Bank loan and keep control of the production of the SC1. You do not want to sub-contract to Electrovans unless Williams resigns. You hate Williams and should be rude to him at the meeting – remember the photograph. You should prepare arguments to support Bellcrest's case (remember Urwin). You should not compromise unless you feel you have to. Remember you hold the patents.

Paul Malone

You should support Downes in his arguments. You, like him, do not want to lose the Bank's money or control of the production of the SC1. Prepare your own arguments in favour of Bellcrest.

Charles Spence

Your prime concern is finance. You should be prepared to show what profit the Bank can expect from investing in Bellcrest rather than Electrovans, and when they can expect a return on their investment.

Electrovans

Donald Williams

You should do everything you can to persuade Sir Frederick to invest in Electrovans rather than Bellcrest, and should prepare arguments to support your case. Remember you are ready to produce a speed control device, Bellcrest are not. Consider whether you want to buy the patents from Bellcrest, or to let Bellcrest sub-contract to you. Does your device infringe the Bellcrest patents?

Harold Wedderburn

You are Electrovans' Marketing Manager. You should prepare arguments to support Electrovans' claim to the Bank's money. You should invent a list of customers who have already ordered speed controls from you to support your case.

Andrew Gordon

You are Electrovans' Company Secretary. You should prepare arguments to support Electrovans' claim to the Bank's money. You should be prepared to show what profit the Bank can expect from investing in Electrovans rather than Bellcrest. andwhen they can expect a return on their investment.

Passlee Electronics

Sam Urwin

You don't care who gets the loan as long as a solution is found. You want your speed controls as soon as possible, and as far as you are concerned this is the point of the meeting. You may propose any compromise you like, including the dismissal of Williams or Downes, if it means that you will get your speed controls quickly.

GLOSSARY

The purpose of the glossary is to help the learner in his reading of the summary, exercises and role-play. Care has been taken to include words which the learner is likely to meet when no recourse to a teacher is possible, e.g. when working at home. Excluded from the glossary are elementary words which the learner is expected to know, e.g. 'employ', 'profit', 'possible', obvious derivatives of known elementary words, e.g. 'employee', 'profitable', 'possibly', words of international currency, e.g. 'deal', 'market', 'computer', and words which occur only in the film. Definitions are restricted to the meanings occurring in the course, e.g. 'back' is defined in the context of 'back a project'. The phonetic transcription used is that of the *English Pronouncing Dictionary* by D. Jones. Alternative pronunciations are not given. The glossary is an aid to the learner but not a dictionary. It should be supplemented where necessary by the use of a good dictionary such as *The Advanced Learner's Dictionary of Current English* by A.S. Hornby, E.V. Gatenby and H. Wakefield.

List of Abbreviations

adj.	adjective	n.	noun
adv.	adverb	prep.	preposition
Am.	American	sb.	somebody
conj.	conjunction	sth.	something
e.g.	for example	v.	verb

abandon	[əˈbændən] v. abandon the plan = give up the plan
A.C.	[ei siː] n. alternating current, flow of electricity in which the positive and negative poles interchange, usually 50 times per second (50 cycles per second) see D.C.
access	[ˈækses] n. have access to information = be able to use information
accordance	[əˈkɔːdəns] n. in accordance with your instructions = according to your instructions
account	[əˈkaunt] n. a bill to be paid; of a firm = accounts department, financial department (see Bellcrest structure plan; bank account = arrangement with a bank to put in and take out money
account	[əˈkaunt] n. take into account = take into consideration
account for	[əˈkaunt fɔː] v. be the reason for, take up; Beamish Motors account for 50% of Electrovans' business.
accurate	[ˈækjurit] adj. exact; accuracy n.
accuse	[əˈkjuːz] v. he accused me of lying = he said I had lied; -ation [ˈækjuˈzeiʃən] n.
achieve	[əˈtʃiːv] v. do sth. successfully; -ment n.
adapt	[əˈdæpt] v. change sth. so that it is more suitable; -ation n.
adequate	[ˈædikwit] adj. enough
adjuster	[əˈdʒʌstə] n. an insurance adjuster = an official of an insurance company who decides the cost of damage

administer	[əd'ministə] v. manage; administration [əd'mini'streiʃən] n.
advance	[əd'vɑːns] v. advance money = lend money
affect	[ə'fekt] v. have an effect on
agenda	[ə'dʒendə] n. list of matters to be discussed at a meeting
agent	['eidʒənt] n. a person who acts for a business; agency n.
air terminal	['ɛə 'təːminl] n. office and bus station for air-passengers; place in town centre where airport buses arrive and depart
allocate	['æləkeit] v. allocate money to/for sth. = allow so much money for a certain purpose
alternative	[ɔːl'təːnətiv] adj. n. a second possibility
announce	[ə'nauns] v. declare; -ment n.
annoy	[ə'nɔi] v. make sb. angry
annual	['ænjuəl] adj. once a year
anticipate	[æn'tisipeit] v. think of sth. before it happens
apologize	[ə'pɔlədʒaiz] v. say you are sorry; apology [ə'pɔlədʒi] n.
apparent	[ə'pærənt] adj. clear
arise	[ə'raiz] v. a complication has arisen = we have just discovered a complication
assess	[ə'ses] v. decide the value of; -ment n.
assume	[ə'sjuːm] v. believe without evidence/facts
assure	[ə'ʃuə] v. say with certainty; I assure you the money will be paid
atmosphere	['ætməsfiə] n. there was an atmosphere of uncertainty = people felt uncertain
attractive	[ə'træktiv] adj. an attractive offer = an advantageous offer
authority	[ɔː'θɔriti] n. airport authority = those in control of the airport
automotive	['ɔːtəu'məutiv] adj. concerned with self-powered vehicles, particularly private cars; the automotive field
available	[ə'veiləbl] adj. money is available = there is money which can be used
aware	[ə'wɛə] adj. be aware of = realize, know
awkward	['ɔːkwəd] adj. causing difficulties
axe	[æks] v. the project was axed = the project was discontinued
back	[bæk] v. support
basis	['beisis] n. starting-point; base [beis] v.
battery	[bætəri] n. object containing metal plates and chemicals for making electricity
benefit	['benifit] v. n. help
Board of Directors	['bɔːd əv di'rektəz] n. group of men controlling a company, elected by and representing the shareholders
bound to	['baund tu] adj. production is bound to suffer = production will certainly suffer
break even	['breik 'iːvn] v. make neither profit nor loss
break off	['breik 'ɔf] v. stop doing sth.
brief	[briːf] n. v. instructions/give instructions; we briefed the new

employee = we told him what to do in his job; -ing n. meeting where sb. is briefed

call off — [ˈkɔːl ˈɔf] v. decide that sth. which has already been arranged will not now happen, e.g. the meeting was called off

campaign — [kæmˈpein] n. a plan of action for a certain purpose e.g. advertising campaign

cancel — [ˈkænsl] v. decide that sth. which has already been arranged will not now happen, e.g. cancel a meeting

capacity — [kəˈpæsiti] n. production capacity = the amount a factory is able to produce

cautious — [ˈkɔːʃəs] adj. not taking risks; caution n.

chairman — [ˈtʃεəmən] n. person in charge of a meeting; chair a meeting

chart — [tʃɑːt] n. a sheet of paper with statistical information, e.g. a sales chart

c.i.f. — [ˌsiː ai ˈef] cost, insurance, freight; the price given includes the cost of the product, insurance, and cost of transport

circumstances — [ˈsəːkəmstænsiz] n. in/under the circumstances = considering the facts

client — [ˈklaiənt] n. a customer

comment — [ˈkɔment] v. say sth. about; comment [ˈkɔment] n.

commission — [kəˈmiʃən] v. appoint sb. to do sth. for you

commission — [kəˈmiʃən] n. money paid to sb. for selling goods

commit oneself — [kəˈmit wʌnself] v. he refused to commit himself = he refused to come to a decision/make his position clear

compensation — [ˌkɔmpənˈseiʃən] n. payment for damage

compete — [kəmˈpiːt] v. try to do better than others; competition [kɔmpəˈtiʃən] competitor [kəmˈpetitə] n. competitive [kəmˈpetitiv] adj.

complication — [ˌkɔmpənˈseiʃən] n. a new difficulty

component — [kəmˈpəunənt] n. part of a complete project

compromise — [ˈkɔmprəmaiz] n. an agreement which settles a problem in an acceptable way although neither side gets everything it wants

concede — [kənˈsiːd] v. concede the point = admit that the other person is right

concentrate on — [ˈkɔnsəntreit ɔn] v. give all one's attention to

conclude — [kənˈkluːd] v. arrive at an opinion; conclusion [kənˈkluːʒən] n. draw a conclusion from the facts

conduct — [kənˈdʌkt] v. conduct a survey = carry out a survey

confidence — [ˈkɔnfidəns] n. we have confidence in his ability = we trust his ability

confidential — [ˌkɔnfiˈdenʃəl] adj. secret; in confidence n.

confirm — [kənˈfəːm] v. remove any doubts

confront — [kənˈfrʌnt] v. come face to face with; -ation [ˌkɔnfrənˈteiʃən] n.

consequence — [ˈkɔnsikwəns] n. a result or effect of sth.

consignment — [kənˈsainmənt] n. goods to be delivered

constant — [ˈkɔnstənt] adj. unchanging

consultant — [kənˈsʌltənt] n. an expert who advises on a particular problem; consult v.

consumer — [kənˈsjuːmə] n. a person who buys/uses goods

content	[kən'tent] adj. satisfied
context	['kɔntekst] n. a word out of context = a word written or said without the rest of the sentence
controversial	[ˌkɔntrə'vəːʃəl] adj. likely to cause disagreement; controversy [kən'trɔvəsi] n.
convenience	[kən'viːnjəns] n. for the sake of convenience = to make things easier
convinced	[kən'vinst] adj. sure; of the firm opinion
co-operate	[kəu'ɔpəreit] v. work together
co-ordinate	[kəu'ɔːdineit] v. to bring into proper relationship, to bring together effectively
corporation	[ˌkɔːpə'reiʃən] n. (Am.) limited company
course	[kɔːs] n. one part of a meal, e.g. soup
create	[kriː'eit] v. make sth. which did not exist/was not there before
current	['kʌrənt] adj. current projects = projects going on at the moment
cut	[kʌt] v. cut production costs = spend less on production; cut down work = do less work; cut out work = stop doing work
deadline	['dedlain] n. final date by which sth. must be done
definite	['definit] adj. certain; -ly adv.
delegation	[ˌdeli'geiʃən] n. group of people acting for a company/government, etc.
deny	[di'nai] v. say that sth. is not true
depart	[di'pɑːt] v. leave, go away; -ure [di'pɑː tʃə] n.
deputy	['depjuti] n. adj. second in command
despatch	[dis'pætʃ] v. send off
device	[di'vais] n. sth. designed for a special purpose
diary	['daiəri] n. book in which daily events are noted
D.C.	['diː'siː] n. direct current, flow of electricity in which positive and negative poles are always the same, see A.C.
disaster	[di'zɑːstə] n. terrible misfortune
disclose	[dis'kləuz] v. make known
discount	['diskaunt] n. amount of money taken off the full price
disgusted	[dis'gʌstid] adj. having a violent feeling of dislike
dismiss	[dis'mis] v. he was dismissed = he was told to leave his job; -al n.
disrupt	[dis'rʌpt] v. throw into disorder
distribute	[dis'tribjut] v. give out, send out; distribution n. distributor n.
diversify	[dai'vəːsifai] enter into new fields, do new types of work; diversification [daiˌvəːsifi'keiʃən] n.
dividend	['dividend] n. regular payment to sb. who has put money into a business
draft	[drɑːft] n. v. rough notes; an outline draft of the report = the first written outline of the report
drawback	['drɔːbæk] n. disadvantage
edge	[edʒ] n. have the edge over a competitor = have an advantage over a competitor
efficient	[i'fiʃənt] adj. able to do sth. well, with the minimum waste of work/time; efficiency n.

emphasize	[ˈemfəsaiz] v. give special importance to; emphasis [ˈemfəsis] n.
enclose	[inˈkləuz] v. I enclose the tickets = I have put the tickets in the envelope
encourage	[inˈkʌridʒ] v. give hope; encouraging adj.
entail	[inˈteil] v. make necessary
entertain	[ˌentəˈtein] v. receive sb. as a guest
entire	[inˈtaiə] adj. complete, whole; -ly adv.
equip	[iˈkwip] v. supply with articles for a special purpose; -ment n.
essential	[iˈsenʃəl] adj. absolutely necessary
establish	[iˈstæbliʃ] v. set up; -ed adj.
eventual	[iˈventʃul] adj. final, in the end; -ly adv.
evidence	[ˈevidəns] n. fact which gives a reason for believing sth.
exaggerate	[igˈzædʒəreit] v. say that sth. is more than it really is
exclude	[iksˈkluːd] v. leave out
exist	[igˈzist] v. be; -ing adj.
expand	[iksˈpænd] v. make larger, grow larger; expansion [iksˈpænʃən] n.
extend	[iksˈtend] v. make longer; extension [iksˈtenʃən] n.
facility	[fəˈsiliti] n. buildings and machines are production facilities, buses and trains are transport facilities
file	[fail] n. the SC1 file = the papers concerning the SC1
finance	[faiˈnæns] n. money
finance	[faiˈnæns] v. supply money for sth; financial adj.
fire brigade	[ˈfaiə briˌgeid] n. men who put out fires
force	[fɔːs] n. group of people, e.g. labour force, sales force
forecast	[ˈfɔːkɑːst] n. v. say what will happen in the future
fork-lift truck	[fɔːk lift ˈtrʌk] n. a vehicle (usually electric) which can lift and lower heavy objects on two metal arms
freight	[freit] n. v. goods, send goods
furious	[ˈfjuəriəs] adj. very angry
gain	[gein] v. win
gasolene	[ˈgæsəliːn] n. (Am.) petrol
get under way	[ˈget ʌndə ˈwei] v. begin
grounds	[graundz] n. on the grounds of expense = because of expense
heading	[ˈhediŋ] n. words coming before each part of a report to show what follows
hold water	[ˈhəuld ˈwɔːtə] v. the argument doesn't hold water = the argument can be shown to be wrong
host	[həust] n. sb. who receives a guest
identify	[aiˈdentifai] v. recognize
ignore	[igˈnɔː] v. take no notice of
imply	[imˈplai] v. suggest
impress	[imˈpres] v. The Board were impressed by the SC1 = the Board formed a

	favourable opinion of the SC1; impressive adj.
incident	[ˈinsidənt] n. event
indicate	[ˈindikeit] v. show
indiscreet	[indisˈkriːt] adj. not careful in what one says (about secret things)
inevitable	[inˈevitəbl] adj. certain to happen
infringe	[inˈfrindʒ] v. infringe a rule = break a rule (infringe a patent)
initiative	[iˈniʃjətiv] n. on his own initiative = without first getting approval
injunction	[in dʒʌŋʃən] n. written order from a law court
insist on	[inˈsist ɔn] v. I insist on immediate payment = I will accept nothing but immediate payment; he insists on coming = no one can stop him coming
instruct	[inˈstrʌkt] v. tell, order
intervene	[ˌintəˈviːn] v. interrupt, to come between two people who are arguing or fighting
invest	[inˈvest] v. put money into a company; -or n. -ment n.
investigate	[inˈvestigeit] v. examine, inquire into
invoice	[ˈinvɔis] n. v. bill for goods or services supplied
involved in	[inˈvɔlvd in] adj. take part in or become part of
issue	[ˈiʃu] n. question, problem
item	[ˈaitəm] n. item on the agenda = one of a list of questions to be discussed
judgement	[ˈdʒʌdʒmənt] n. ability to decide, make a decision
labour	[ˈleibə] n. work
launch	[lɔːnʃ] v. launch a product = put a product on the market, start selling a product
licensing agreement	[ˈlaisənsiŋ əˌgriːmənt] n. contract/agreement to let another company produce your goods under licence in return for payment
life-cycle	[ˈlaif ˈsaikl] n. (of a product) time during which a product sells well enough to be worth producing and selling
link	[liŋk] n. v. connection
liquidity	[liˈkwiditi] n. availability of cash to make payment, rather than credit on assets e.g. property, equipment etc.
maintain	[meinˈtein] v. keep, look after equipment, buildings
maintain	[meinˈtein] v. hold an opinion
major	[ˈmeidʒə] adj. chief, very important
manoeuvrability	[məˌnuːvrəˈbiliti] n. ability to be moved in a small space
manufacture	[ˌmænjuˈfæktʃə] v. make, produce
mechanism	[ˈmekənizm] n. machine
memo	[ˈmeməu] n. a note sent to another person, usually in the same company. It does not carry an address, greetings etc, like a letter
merchant bank	[ˈməːtʃənt ˈbæŋk] n. trading bank
merely	[ˈmiəli] adv. only
merge	[məːdʒ] v. join together to become one; merger n.

a joining of two or more companies

mess [mes] n. state of disorder

minimize ['minimaiz] v. make as small as possible

minute ['minit] n. minutes of a meeting = official written records of what was said at a meeting

motion ['məuʃən] n. a suggestion or proposal to be discussed and voted on at a meeting

moreover [mɔː'rəuvə] adv. in addition

negotiate [ni'gəuʃieit] v. discuss, in order to reach an agreement

obliged to [ə'blaidʒd tu] adj. he was obliged to explain the position = he had to explain the position

obstruct [əb'strʌkt] v. be in the way, make difficulties; -ive adj.

obtain [əb'tein] v. get for oneself

occur [ə'kəː] v. happen

operation [ˌɔpə'reiʃən] n. activity

outlet ['autlet] n. sales outlet = place where goods are sold to the public, e.g. a shop, an agency

output ['autput] n. amount of production; weekly output of a factory = the quantity produced by the factory in a week

outstanding [aut'stændiŋ] adj. not yet completed

overlap [ˌəuvə'læp] v. our duties overlap = our duties are partly the same

overlook [ˌəuvə'luk] v. fail to see

participate [pɑː'tisipeit] v. take part in

percentage [pə'sentidʒ] n. the number per hundred

perform [pə'fɔːm] v. do; the SC1 performed excellently; -ance n.

persist in [pə'sist in] v. keep on doing sth; he persisted in arguing with the directors = he kept on arguing with the directors

persuade [pə'sweid] v. reason with sb; in order to make him do sth.

point [pɔint] n. fact or idea mentioned in discussion; raise a point = introduce a new thought for consideration

policy ['pɔlisi] n. general aims

policy ['pɔlisi] n. contract of insurance

pollution [pə'ljuːʃən] n. making one's surroundings dirty

postpone [pəus'pəun] v. put off to a later date

potential [pə'tenʃəl] adj. possible

precedent ['presidənt] n. set a precedent = set an example for the future

preliminary [pri'liminəri] adj. done first as a preparation

premium ['priːmjəm] n. amount paid for insurance

previous ['priːvjəs] adj. earlier

primary ['praiməri] adj. first, most important; primarily adv.

principal ['prinsipl] adj. chief, most important

principle ['prinsipl] n. in principle = in general

prior ['praiə] adj. earlier in time, earlier in order

priority	[prai'ɔriti] n. the greatest importance
proceed	[prə'si:d] v. go forward
process	['prəuses] v. data processing = arranging information usually with a computer
production line	[prə'dʌkʃən lain] n. the men and machinery taking part in production
product line	['prɔdʌkt lain] n. type of product
project	['prodʒekt] n. plan for development
promote	[prə'məut] v. promote greater understanding = work for greater understanding; move up into a better job
propose	[prə'pəuz] v. suggest; proposal n.
prospect	['prɔspekt] n. possibility for the future
protest	['prəutest] n. a strong objection; protest [prə'test] v.
prototype	['prəutəutaip] n. the first model to be developed
publicity	[pʌ'blisiti] n. it was given a lot of publicity = everyone heard or read about it; a publicity agent = sb. paid to organise advertisements
punctual	['pʌŋtʃul] adj. not late, on time
purchase	[pə:tʃəs] v. n. buy; sth. that is bought
put up	['put 'ʌp] v. he put up a proposal = he made a proposal, he put forward a proposal
qualify	['kwɔlifai] v. pass a test; he is a qualified engineer = he has been trained and has passed an examination as an engineer; qualification [ˌkwɔlifi'keiʃən] n.
questionnaire	['kwestʃə'nεə] n. a list of questions to be answered, used for the purpose of getting information on a subject
quote	[kwəut] v. repeat the exact words sb. has used
quote the price	['kwəut ðə 'prais] v. name the price; quotation [kwəu'teiʃən] n.
radiator	['reidieitə] n. radiator of a car = the part where the water is cooled
ratio	['reiʃiəu] n. cost-price ratio = the relationship between the cost and the price
reaction	[ri:'ækʃən] n. I don't know what his reaction was = I don't know what effect it had on him; react v.
reassure	[ˌri:ə'ʃuə] v. tell sb. that there is no need to worry; reassurance n.
recharge	['ri:'tʃɑ:dʒ] v. recharge a battery = put electricity back into a battery
record	['rekɔ:d] n. a written account of sth; record [ri'kɔ:d] v.
recover	[ri'kʌvə] v. get better get back sth. which was lost; recovery n.
reduce	[ri'dju:s] v. make smaller, make less; reduction [ri 'dʌkʃən] n.
reject	[ri'dʒekt] v. decide against, refuse to accept; rejection n.
relevant	['relivənt] adj. related to the subject under consideration; relevance n.
reluctant	[ri'lʌktənt] adj. not very willing; reluctance n.
rely on	[ri'lai ɔn] v. depend on; reliable adj.
replace	[ri:'pleis] v. we'll have to replace this old machinery = we'll have to buy

some new machinery to use in place of the old; replacement n.

'epresent — [ˌrepriˈzent] v. he represents Bellcrest = he acts for Bellcrest; this represents an improvement = this is a sign of improvement; representative adj.

'eputation — [ˌrepjuˈteiʃən] n. they have a good reputation = it is the general opinion that they are good; reputable [ˈrepjutəbl] adj.

'equire — [riˈkwaiə] v. need; requirement n.

esearch — [riˈsəːtʃ] n. study of a subject so as to discover new facts

esign — [riˈzain] v. give up one's job; resignation [ˌrezigˈneiʃən] n. a letter of resignation

esistor — [riˈzistə] n. a means of changing a flow of electricity into heat

esolve — [ˌriˈzolv] v. decide
resolve an argument = put an end to the argument; resolution [ˌrezəˈljuːʃən] n. formal decision reached at a meeting

esources — [riˈzɔːsiz] n. money, supplies etc. available for use

esponsible — [risˈpɔnsəbl] adj. he is responsible for that = it is his duty to do that; responsibility [risˈpɔnsəˈbiliti] n. a position of responsibility = a position where decisions must be taken

etain — [riˈtein] v. keep; retention [riˈtenʃən] n.

eturns — [riˈtəːnz] n. profit

eveal — [riˈviːl] v. he revealed the secret = he let the secret be known

eview — [riˈvjuː] v. n. examine, look carefully at

evise — [riˈvaiz] v. change so as to improve, reconsider; revision [riˈviʒən] n.

evive — [riˈvaiv] v. bring back into use; revival n.

ig up — [ˈrig ˈʌp] v. you must rig up a demonstration = you must arrange a demonstration

ival — [ˈraivl] n. a person or company that wants to do better than you; rivalry n.

umour — [ˈruːmə] n. there have been rumours about it = people have been saying things about it but nobody knows if these things are true

un down — [ˈrʌn ˈdaun] v. run down production = produce less

arcastic — [sɑːˈkæstik] adj. speaking in a cruel way
sarcasm [ˈsɑːkæzm] n. cruelly or bitterly worded, in a bitter or cruel voice

ceptical — [ˈskeptikl] adj. finding it difficult to believe; scepticism [ˈskeptisizm] n.

cope — [skəup] n. scope for discussion = opportunity for discussion; it is outside the scope of the report = it is not inside the area of the report

creen — [skriːn] n. an object used for showing photographs, e.g. a film screen

econd — [ˈsekənd] v. second a motion = allow your name to be used to show that you support the suggestion put forward by another, to speak in favour of the suggestion put forward

econd-rate — [ˈsekəndˈreit] adj. not the best, not first class

ector — [ˈsektə] n. an area of industry, e.g. private vehicle sector

ecurity — [siˈkjuəriti] n. safety; the security officer = person in charge of safety arrangements

select	[si'lekt] v. choose; selection [si'lekʃən] n.
senior	['siːnjə] adj. a senior member of staff = one who holds a high position
series	['siəriːz] n. a number of things each related to the one before, e.g. 1, 2, 3, 4 is a series of numbers
setback	['setbæk] n. a difficulty or problem which stops progress
share	[ʃɛə] n. he has shares in oil = he has put money into an oil company and gets part of the profits; shareholder n.
site	[sait] n. place where sth. will be built
soak	[səuk] v. make very wet
sole	[səul] adj. only
solve	[sɔlv] v. find an answer; solution [sə'luːʃən] n.
sound	[saund] adj. safe, not taking risks
source	[sɔːs] n. place where sth. originates
specifications	[ˌspesifi'keiʃənz] n. detailed plan for the design of sth.
staff	[stɑːf] n. employees working for a company
stage	[steidʒ] n. at this stage = now, at this time in the development
state	[steit] v. say, declare; -ment n.
stock	[stɔk] n. goods held in store stocktake ['stɔkˌteik] v. check the stock
strain	[strein] v. overstretch; strain the resources = do sth. for which the resources are hardly enough
stress	[stres] v. give importance to
strict	[strikt] adj. clear and exact
sub-contract	[ˌsʌb'kɔntrækt] n. a contract with a company for carrying out work which that company has already contracted to do; sub-contract [ˌsʌbkən'trækt] v.
subject to	['sʌbdʒikt tu] prep. dependent on
submit	[səb'mit] v. submit a report = put a report forward to be discussed
subsidiary	[səb'sidjəri] adj. n. a subsidiary company is controlled by another company.
sufficient	[sə'fiʃənt] adj. enough
summary	['sʌməri] n. a short report which includes only the most important things
supplement	['sʌplimənt] n. addition to sth.
surge diverter	['səːdʒ dai'vəːtə] n. a device for protecting electrical equipment from a sudden flow of electricity
survey	['səːvei] n. a systematic enquiry; survey [səː'vei] v.
suspend	[səs'pend] v. stop doing sth. for the moment
switch	[switʃ] v. n. change
tackle	[tækl] v. tackle a problem = deal with a problem
take aback	['teik ə'bæk] v. he was taken aback = he was very surprised
take over	['teik 'əuvə] v. get control of; takeover ['teikˌəuvə] n.
term	[təːm] n. length of time; long-term profits = profits received after a long time
terminate	['təːmineit] v. finish

terms	[tə:mz] n. in terms of = with regard to; terms of reference = exact description of a subject to be dealt with; terms of payment = conditions of payment
tie down	[ˈtai ˈdaun] v. tie sb. down = limit his freedom of action, make him promise to do sth.
tough	[tʌf]adj. hard to cut and eat
transfer	[træns'fə:] v. change, move; transfer['trænsfə:] n.
turn down	[ˈtə:n ˈdaun] v. turn down an offer = refuse an offer
tyre	[taiə] n. rubber air-filled covering on a car wheel
undertake	[ˌʌndəˈteik] v. agree to do, start work on
underwrite	[ˈʌndərait] v. agree to pay the cost of insurance claims; -r n.
utmost	[ˈʌtməust] adj. n. the greatest possible
vacant	[ˈveikənt] adj. empty; fill a vacancy = appoint someone to a job
vary	[ˈvɛəri] v. change, be different; variable adj.
vehicle	[ˈvi:ikl] n. means of transport by road, e.g. car, bus
vital	[ˈvaitl] adj. of the greatest importance
volume	[ˈvɔljum] n. amount
warehouse	[ˈwɛəhaus] n. a building for storing goods
water	[ˈwɔ:tə] see – 'hold water'
whereas	[wɛərˈæz] conj. on the other hand
whole-hearted	[ˈhəulˈhɑ:tid] adj. he gave me his whole-hearted support; -ly adv.
windscreen	[ˈwindskri:n] n. front window of a car
withdraw	[wiðˈdrɔ:] v. withdraw a loan = take away a loan; -al n.
within	[wiˈðin] prep. prep. within a week = before the end of seven days
worthwhile	[ˈwə:θˈwail] adj. worth doing

KEY TO THE WRITTEN EXERCISES

EPISODE 1

Exercise A

1 An *investor* is a man who puts his money into a business. If he *invests* his money in a company, he usually buys *shares* in that company, and is known as a *shareholder*. Instead of a fixed *rate* of *interest* he usually receives a *dividend* on his capital.

2 Unless a company holds a monopoly, it has to *compete* with rival firms. The existence of *competition* is a factor no company can ignore; indeed many companies keep a constant eye on the activities of their *competitors*.

3 Before a company decides to produce a new product, it must ensure that there is a *market* for it. To find out whether it can *market* the product, a company will often conduct a *market survey/study*. Most companies have a *Marketing Manager* who is in charge of sales promotion.

Exercise B

1 Orpenshaw works in the Research and Development Department.
2 Downes carries heavy responsibility.
3 Evans isn't on the Board of Directors.
4 Does Bellcrest manufacture electronic components?
5 Ashburnham doesn't want to continue the loan to Bellcrest.
6 When do you want my report?
7 Downes doesn't understand Needham's arguments.
8 He delays every decision until it's too late.
9 Do you have/have you got plans for development?
10 We don't know why our products don't sell.

Exercise C

1 Five years ago Smith & Co. only *manufactured* bicycles.
2 They always *sold* most of their products on the home market but *exported* some of them to Africa.
3 In 1968 foreign competition *increased* and sales *dropped* sharply.
4 The Board of Directors *felt* that the company *had to* diversify.
5 They *planned* to get a loan from the bank, and as the company *enjoyed* a high reputation, they *had* no difficulty in getting one.
6 They *spent* this money on development and *began* production of motorcycles a few weeks ago.
7 Hanson *wrote* a very interesting article on Bellcrest.
8 Bellcrest *took over* a smaller company last year.
9 Their competitors *read* about it in the Financial Times.
10 Our customer *bought up* our complete stock.

EPISODE 2

Exercise A

1 Downes, Spence and Malone met to *discuss* the threatened withdrawal of the loan. A *proposal* to revive the SC1 was put forward. A number of important points had to be *taken* into *account* before a *decision* could be reached. Malone was in *favour* of the SC1, but Spence was very much *against* it and raised several *objections*. Spence and Malone had an *argument* over the advantages and *disadvantages* of the SC1, and it was clear

that the matter was going to need careful *consideration.* In the end, Downes *agreed* to keep an open mind on the SC1.

2 Five years ago the SC1 was *suspended.* Williams, who was in charge of the project, felt that it was being *abandoned* and left the company. Nobody was quite sure if he had *resigned* or been *dismissed.*

Exercise B

1 There will be sharp competition from other companies.
2 It is likely to strain our production resources.
3 There will be a period when we don't show a profit.
4 There will be many people who think the project is too ambitious.
5 There is an expanding market in the automotive field.
6 There will be a big increase in the use of electric vehicles in the next five years.
7 It is true that we must make a careful market study.
8 It will be possible to reduce production costs by designing-in cheaper components.
9 There are good sales opportunities for a variable speed control mechanism.
10 There is enough money in the budget for a market study.

Exercise C

Malone told Jean to get Orpenshaw on the phone. Malone asked/told Orpenshaw to come up to his office straight away. Malone told Orpenshaw he wanted to discuss development projects. Orpenshaw offered to bring all the results of the market study on the BX3 with him. Malone advised Orpenshaw to put all that in writing. Orpenshaw agreed/promised/decided to write a full report. Malone wanted/told Orpenshaw to give it to Evans by the end of the week. Orpenshaw agreed/promised to have it ready by Thursday. Malone arranged to meet again on Friday morning. Malone asked Orpenshaw to be there at ten. Malone told Jean to put that in his diary.

Exercise D

I know that the SC1 has Malone's *whole-hearted* support, but I must say, Maurice, I feel *doubtful* about the whole project. Of course, the design of the SC1 is *technically* advanced but Bellcrest has no *immediate* experience of selling to the *private* vehicle sector. This is a *highly* competitive field and my big fear is that we may not be able to produce the goods as *efficiently* as our rivals. It might be difficult for us to take advantage of the *potential* market. I am *primarily* concerned with the cost of this project. Production costs for the SC1 would be *high* so we cannot expect an *immediate* profit. I think the BX3 project would be much more *suitable.*

EPISODE 3

Exercise A

1 Malone wanted to be quite sure that there was a *potential* market for the SC1, so he decided to *commission* a market *survey/study.* He called in a firm of *Management Consultants* who were *specialists* in marketing.

2 Some time ago Bellcrest invested a considerable amount in new buildings and machinery, so their *production facilities* are now first-class. However, a new *product line* like the SC1 would put a strain on their *production resources*. It was necessary to plan immediately so that the *production capacity* of their factory could be increased. Bellcrest still had many *product lines* which had not yet reached the end of their *life cycles.*

3 a Development of the BX10 was stopped because it was too *expensive.*
b We'll have to buy the BX13 from Bellcrest although it's *priced* rather high.
c Spence opposed the SC1 on the grounds of *expense.*
d Do you know the *cost* of raw materials?
e Our *expenditure* on marketing has increased over the last year.
f We had to make price increases because of the *cost* of labour.
g We can't spend so much on development if we're going to *cover* our *costs.*
h The manufacturers won't buy these components if the *price* is too high.
i After taking a visitor from Electrovans out to lunch, Mr Malone claimed *expenses* from Bellcrest.
j We'll have to *cost* the development of this product line very carefully.

Exercise B

1 Bellcrest's Sales Manager used to work for Davidson's before.
2 An experienced salesman is used to dealing with awkward questions.
3 Our Managing Director used to be against this project.
4 This mechanism is used to control the speed of the vehicle.
5 M.P. Consultants are used to preparing market surveys in the automotive field.
6 Sometimes a bank loan is used to finance new production facilities.
7 Beverman and Jones used to export components to Germany ten years ago.
8 Fork-lift trucks are used to carry the goods to the store.
9 Malone is used to submitting reports to Downes by now.
10 Modern production lines are used to increase production capacity.

Exercise D

Malone: Right, Dennis, let's get down to business. Now, what about this market study. Which of the management consultant firms *should* we go to.

Evans: Management consultants? Is that really necessary? *Wouldn't* it be possible to do that ourselves?

Malone: Oh, no, Dennis. This job is far too big for us. It *should* be done by an outside firm. It *wouldn't* do to make any mistakes, *would* it.

Evans: Well, in that case, I think M.P. Consultants *would* be the best people to go to. After all, they're specialists in marketing, so they *should* be able to answer all our questions.

Malone: How long *should* we give them to complete the study?

Evans: Well, that rather depends on how soon we want it. It *shouldn't* take them long. They're very efficient. They *should* manage to get it done by the end of the month. I think my assistant *should* go and see them in person. The chief consultant is a friend of his. If he explained the position, they *would* probably give it priority.

EPISODE 4

Exercise A

1 Beeston left the Ministry of Defence because there seemed to be little *prospect* of ever rising to a higher position. He had been there five years and had not been *promoted.* Beamish Motors had several *vacancies* to *fill* and they *offered* him a *job* at a high salary, with good *prospects* for *promotion.* After he had signed the *contract* of *employment* he found out that he was stuck behind a desk all day doing boring routine paperwork. He wanted more job *satisfaction* so he asked the management if he could *transfer* to one of their subsidiary companies.

2 Urwin came over from Canada to re-negotiate the *licensing agreement/ arrangement* between Passlee Electronics and Bellcrest. Under the *terms* of this *agreement/arrangement* Passlee is allowed to manufacture Bellcrest products in Canada. This does not, however, prevent them from *negotiating contracts* with other companies.

3 Bellcrest commissioned M.P. Consultants to conduct a preliminary *survey/ study* on the market prospects for the SC1. Their instructions were laid down in the *brief* that Malone sent to Dr Perkins. Their *terms* of *reference* included industrial vehicles, commercial vehicles, and electrically driven private vehicles. These were the three *areas* that interested Bellcrest and they asked the consultants to organize their report under these *headings.* The company had already gathered some facts on the use of cars in cities and they offered to give Bellcrest the *data/details.* As Bellcrest did not want anyone to know about their revived interest in the SC1, they asked the consultants to *treat* the matter as *confidential.*

Exercise B

1 If Urwin visits Electrovans, he will enquire about vehicle components.
2 Electrovans will hear about the SC1 if Malone informs Urwin.
3 If Malone does not inform Urwin, Passlee Electronics will buy from a competitor.
4 Electrovans will compete with Bellcrest, if they enter the private vehicle sector.
5 Bellcrest will need a product executive if they develop the SC1.
6 Bellcrest should appoint Beeston if the Board approves the new post.
7 Bellcrest should treat the project as confidential if other companies compete.
8 If Electrovans produce a speed control mechanism, Bellcrest should examine the patents carefully.
9 Bellcrest should get finance from other sources if the Bank refuses to renew the loan.
10 If the consultants confirm their fears, Bellcrest should accept the facts.

Exercise C

Malone is worried because Urwin *is visiting* Electrovans to have a look at their vehicle components. He *doesn't want* to tell Urwin that Bellcrest *are moving* into the field of vehicle components. Buf if he *doesn't tell* Urwin about the SC1, he will risk Urwin buying from Electrovans. He also *thinks* Williams *is trying* to get Orpenshaw away from Bellcrest. Malone *takes* the problems to Downes who suggests it is Urwin who *is trying* to take Orpenshaw from Bellcrest and if he *succeeds* there will be no chance of developing the SC1. Downes *settles* the matter by telling Malone not to inform Urwin of Bellcrest's plans.

Exercise D

1 Other companies have already shown interest in this market.
2 Has the Ministry of Defence drawn up the terms of the contract yet?
3 We have never sold components in the private vehicle sector before.
4 Orpenshaw hasn't decided to accept the offer of a new job yet.
5 Have you ever thought of changing your job?
6 Since 1965 Bellcrest have renewed the patents annually.
7 There has never been any consumer demand for electrically driven cars.
8 Hanson has just written a series of articles on the motor industry.
9 The Directors have almost finished discussing Malone's report on the SC1.
10 Hasn't Malone told Urwin about Bellcrest's development plans yet?

EPISODE 5

Exercise A

1 When people go out they often go to a *restaurant.* If they're taking a guest they often *book* a *table* in advance as in popular restaurants it is sometimes difficult to get a table without a *reservation.* On arrival a *waiter* leads them to a table and brings them a *menu.* Many restuarants have a *wine waiter,* who brings them the *wine list* to show them what there is to drink. It is usual to order the first two *courses* together, and further *courses* later in the meal. At the end of the meal a *bill* will be brought.

2 A car runs on *petrol* If you're in England you get *petrol* at a *petrol station,* known in America as a *gasolene station.* The *attendant* is the man who serves you. He will usually clean the *windscreen* and *back window* for you while you are waiting. If you ask him, he will also *top up* the *radiator* with water, the *battery* with distilled water, check that your *tyres* are at the right pressure and that you have sufficient *oil.*

Exercise B

1 Downes stopped the SC1 project when he took over five years ago.
2 Orpenshaw was working on the SC1 project when Downes stopped it.
3 Urwin was just leaving when Malone received a telephone call.
4 Dr Perkins phoned Malone while he was interviewing Beeston.
5 Malone was entertaining Urwin when he heard the news of the fire.
6 Malone phoned Downes when he heard the news of the fire.
7 When Downes rang Ashburnham, he found they were still considering withdrawing the loan.
8 Hanson visited Bellcrest because he was writing a series of articles.
9 Malone was dictating letters when Evans dropped in.
10 Urwin rang Malone while he was waiting at a petrol station.

Exercise C

Downes: Yes. The Minister *is coming* here next Tuesday. He *is arriving* on the 10.30 train.

Malone: Have you any plans for the visit? What *is* he *going to do* when he gets here?

Downes: Well, we have made one or two plans. We *are going to show* him round the new factory first.

Malone: Right, I *will see* that all that stuff left by the builders is cleared up.

Downes: Yes, please do. Oh, and make sure that those electric wires are properly fixed.

Malone: Heavens, yes! I had forgotten about that. Don't worry, I *will have* a word with the chief electrician immediately.

Downes: He *is going to talk* to some of the workers on the production line. It's a bit difficult to say how long this *will take* – possibly about an hour and a half. Then we *are having* lunch with members of the Board at 12.30. By the way, I haven't done anything about flowers for the table.

Malone: Oh, I have already talked to Jean about that, and she *is going to look after* that.

Downes: Good. Then at two o'clock we *are meeting* to discuss Government plans to promote exports. They say they *are going to help* companies that want to expand their export market. If we can convince them that our development projects are sound, they *will support* us financially.

Malone: Look. Orpenshaw says he *is going to conduct* tests on the SC1 prototype next week. I'd like the Minister to see that.

Downes: Oh, yes. I promise you we *will show* him that.

Malone: When is he due to leave?

Downes: He *is travelling* to London on the 4.30 train.

Exercise D

1 No, and I'd prefer him not to know for the moment.
2 Yes, I'd like to persuade him to stay.
3 No, I don't expect to finish it until next week.
4 No, I don't want to give them details yet.
5 No, I'd prefer not to consult him about this matter.
6 I'm not sure but I hope to see him before he leaves.
7 No, I don't expect him to cause any trouble.
8 Yes. I wouldn't like them to withdraw the loan.
9 I'm afraid not. I don't expect to get them until the end of the month.
10 No, I'd prefer not to speak to them till tomorrow.

Exercise E

a *Accepting:*
Maurice Downes has great pleasure in accepting the Chairman and Board of Directors' kind invitation to the reception on Wednesday 3rd April 1972.

b *Refusing:*
Maurice Downes regrets that he is unable to accept the Chairman and Board of Directors' kind invitation to the reception on Wednesday 3rd April 1972, due to a previous engagement.

EPISODE 6

Exercise A 1 Needham was very concerned about whether the warehouse destroyed in the fire had been *insured.* Downes told him that the building had been *insured for* £50,000, and that the *policy* also *covered* the stocks in the building. He told Needham that Bellcrest paid the *insurance company* a high *premium.* The following day the *insurance adjuster* came to discuss Bellcrest's *claim* for the damage caused by the fire.

2 Spence told the meeting that Bellcrest would be short of cash for several weeks. He gave a number of reasons for this *short-term liquidity* problem. Firstly, Bellcrest would not get *compensation* from the insurance company immediately, as it would take time for the *insurance underwriters* to meet the claim. Secondly, the company would not be able to *invoice* customers, as there would be no goods being delivered. At the same time, he had to secure a short-term *cash flow* to meet extra wage bills for overtime.

Exercise B 1a The fire brigade had to prevent the fire from spreading.

b Driver will have to find additional storage space.

c The firemen had to soak the R & D area.

d Malone had to phone Downes immediately.

e Spence will have to put in a claim to the insurance company.

f Miss Banks had to interview Downes.

g Malone will have to visit customers in Europe.

h The press had to take photographs of the fire.

i Orpenshaw will have to tidy up the mess as soon as he can.

j Downes had to stay up most of the night.

2

Downes: I'm afraid the damage is very serious. Production *is bound to* be affected and we *are bound to* be very short of storage space.

Needham: Do you mean you'll *be obliged to* find storage space outside the factory.

Downes: Yes, I think we'll have to. And all the staff will *be obliged to* work overtime until we're on our feet again. Also, the fire *is bound to* delay the research work considerably.

Needham: Yes, I was just talking to Orpenshaw, who has *been obliged to* tidy up the mess over there.

Exercise C Dear Mr. Malone,

<u>Alan Beeston</u>

Thank you for your letter of 8th July 1971.

Mr Beeston *came* to us last October on a year's contract. During his time here he *has shown* considerable ability in his work and *has been* a useful member of our team. He *took* a degree in electronic engineering at Manchester University eight years ago and *joined* the Ministry of Defence when he *left* University. His experience in negotiating contracts for the Ministry *has been* very valuable in his work here.

I *have known* Mr Beeston for five years and my experience of him leads me to believe that the work he *did* at the Ministry after leaving university and the excellent work he *has already done* for us make him first class material for a post such as technical salesman or product executive.

Yours sincerely,

Peter Barker
Personnel Manager

EPISODE 7

Exercise A

1 Most companies employ a number of *salesmen* to sell their products. Collectively, they are known as the *sales force* and they come under the direction of the *Sales Manager.* Occasionally it is necessary for a company to launch a *sales campaign*, also known as a *sales drive*, in order to promote sales of a particular product. In such a campaign, the salesmen look for new *sales outlets* for the product, which means finding new customers.

2 Western Telecommunications buy their components from Bellcrest, and they do this according to a *schedule* in order to ensure regular *deliveries*. On arrival, the components are added to existing *stocks* held by the company. Information concerning components delivered and issued from stock is fed into a computer, which maintains *stock control*, and can give accurate information on *stock levels* at any time. Before they bought the computer, Dobson, as Head Storeman, had to count the components himself every month, which made *stock-taking* an extremely tiresome job.

3 When a new invention is made, the inventor usually *applies* for a *patent* to stop other people from copying his design. Once it has been *taken out,* the law protects the patent from being *infringed* by others.

Exercise B

1 Malone told Jean to get the travel documents.
2 Malone told Jean he would make the travel arrangements himself.
3 Downes told Miss Armstrong he would book his own hotel room.
4 Orpenshaw told Malone he had refused the job.
5 Malone told his secretary to take a letter.
6 Driver told Downes that he would need extra storage space.
7 Spence told Downes that there would be a short-term liquidity problem.
8 Malone told Jean he would arrange his own flights.
9 Malone told Jean to arrange the flights.
10 Downes told Miss Armstrong to telephone Sir Frederick.

Exercise C

1 I look forward *to hearing* from you.
2 We couldn't prevent them *from turning* to Electrovans.
3 Would you mind *waiting* a moment?
4 We are interested *in buying* 500 of your Model YZ camera.
5 I don't see the point *in/of discussing* this question at this stage.
6 These measures will enable us *to increase* production.
7 We are relying *on receiving* the goods by the end of the week.
8 I haven't finished *drawing up* my proposals yet.

9 Did you remember *to bring* that report, Miss Smith?
10 You don't seem *to understand* what I'm saying.
11 He suggested *re-scheduling* our deliveries.
12 He insists *on seeing* you personally, sir.

EPISODE 8

Exercise A

1 When Malone visited Paris he found Picard *disappointed* at Bellcrest's inability to deliver according to schedule. Picard *appreciated* Bellcrest's difficulties, but as the delay put him in an *unpleasant* position, he insisted that the components he had ordered were needed *urgently. Happily* for Malone, Dr Lang was only too *pleased* to return five thousand of the components Picard needed. This was *lucky* for Malone, and he was very *grateful* to Dr Lang, as he would have lost Picard's custom if he hadn't been able to meet his order.

2 Malone couldn't understand why Dr Lang's order had been delayed, as it had been *despatched* from England by *air freight* a month previously. He therefore telephoned his *agent,* Heinlein. Heinlein told him that the *consignment* had not been *cleared* by customs, as Bellcrest had not sent sufficient copies of the *invoice.* He also told Malone that he was arranging for Picard's order to be sent on by his *forwarding agent* to Paris.

Exercise B

1 I'll have to look through the file before I see Spence.
2 I'll have to negotiate a contract when the buyer comes.
3 I'll have to think about production of the SC1 before I speak to Driver.
4 I'll have to leave the RN2 question until I have lunch with Downes.
5 I'll have to book theatre seats before Janet phones.
6 I'll have to read the agenda before I attend the meeting.
7 I'll have to invite Urwin to dinner when I ring him.
8 I'll have to review past developments when I write the SC1 report.
9 I'll have to brief Evans before we visit M.P. Consultants.
10 I'll have to keep quiet about Orpenshaw until Urwin comes to dinner.

Exercise C

1 Urwin admitted to Malone that he found Williams very interesting.
2 Spence warned the committee that the insurance company would not meet the claim immediately.
3 Malone explained to Janet that Bellcrest had to keep quiet about the SC1.
4 M.P. Consultants told Bellcrest that they thought there was now a market for the SC1.
5 Spence pointed out that the Bank did not know anything about the development plans.
6 Janet mentioned to her husband that Williams wanted to find out about the SC1.
7 Evans assured his customers that Bellcrest would increase production as soon as possible.
8 Heinlein informed Malone that the D.A.U. company was expanding fast.
9 Orpenshaw warned Malone that Electrovans intended to produce a speed control device.
10 Dr Lang told Malone that his firm did not require the ZA24 transistors. .

Exercise D

Malone: Unfortunately most of our stocks *were destroyed* last week when a fire *broke* out in our factory.

Lang: Yes, I *heard* about it. Several European companies *buy* regularly from Bellcrest and your products *are valued* in Germany. The fire *was reported* in our newspapers.

Malone: Some of the reports in the English papers *exaggerated* the extent of the damage. They *did not mention* that production *will/would be increased* in the near future. Of course, deliveries *will be delayed* to a certain extent.

Lang: Actually, at the moment I am more worried about our last order from Bellcrest. The consignment *was expected* about three weeks ago but it *has failed* to arrive up to now.

Malone: That's very strange. It *was air freighted* on the second of the month. I *will speak* to our agent about it immediately and I hope the matter *will be settled* to your satisfaction.

Exercise E

TO JEAN PICARD STOP QUINZE RUE LAMARTINE
STOP PARIS DIX-SEPTIEME

IMMEDIATE DESPATCH COMPONENTS EX GERMANY
STOP EXPECTED ARRIVAL BY FRIDAY STOP PARIS
AGENT DUPIERRE WILL INFORM STOP LETTER
FOLLOWS STOP MALONE STOP

This is an example and should not be treated as the only possible telegram.

EPISODE 9

Exercise A

1 Ashburnham and Needham discussed whether to support Bellcrest or Electrovans. Needham felt that Electrovans were more *adventurous* than Bellcrest, and that the company was a *forward-looking* concern. Williams, he said, had *pushe ahead* with development whereas Downes had been more cautious.
Sir Frederick felt that Electrovans *lacked* the *soundness* of Bellcrest and were too *dependent* on one or two large customers. Needham replied that that was the reason why Williams wanted capital to *break free* and *finance expansion.* Without this capital, he couldn't *afford* to.

2 When Malone visited M.P. Consultants he was shown some *statistics* on the *data* Sherwood and Dean had collected. The *statistics* showed the principal manufacturers of electric vehicles and their *volume* of *production.* Malone was shown a *chart* on a screen indicating the *growth* in production and the *total production* of electric vehicles over the past twenty years. To get this information, M.P. Consultants had sent *questionnaires* to manufacturers.
A lot of the data on potential customers was not included in their *preliminary study/survey,* as the *preliminary findings* were outside its *scope.*

Exercise B

1 Living at home is more comfortable than staying in/at a second-rate hotel.

3 Making a statement is simpler than giving interviews.
4 Meeting orders is more satisfactory than asking customers to accept delays.
5 Soaking papers with water is worse than burning them.
6 Making components ourselves is more expensive than buying (them) from Bellcrest.
7 Financing new developments is more progressive than looking for quick profits.
8 Finding markets is harder than planning production.
9 Approaching potential customers is more adventurous than waiting for them to approach us.
10 Commissioning a survey is safer than listening to rumours.

Exercise C

Perkins: We sent out questionnaires to *a lot of* firms that already use electric vehicles.

Malone: Did *many* of them reply.

Perkins: About 40%, which is quite *a lot* compared with other surveys. *More* than half of these companies felt that there would not be *much* advantage in increased mileage if this raised the cost of the vehicle. Only 25% of them felt it would be worth paying *more* for increased mileage.

Malone: 25%! That's not *many.*

Perkins: I'm afraid we haven't been able to find out *much* about potential users of electric vehicles although we questioned *a lot of* companies in the private vehicle sector. There seems to be *more* interest abroad than in the U.K. I think you would get quite *a lot of* support from European companies. But at the moment there are not *many* British manufacturers interested in developing an electric car. Of course, there have been rumours that Cremorne Cars tried to develop an electric city car but dropped the project because they couldn't get the right kind of AC speed control. Unfortunately, they won't confirm these rumours, so we haven't *much* to go on in the way of hard facts. However, we will try to get *more* information about this.

Exercise D

Sir Frederick: Downes is a sound businessman *in spite of* his reluctance to take risks. I know he abandoned a lot of development projects *while* getting Bellcrest back on its feet again, but this was necessary if the company was to remain in business. And he did a very good job, *although* forcing Williams to resign was perhaps a mistake. Downes has increased profits *while* still maintaining a high level of technical excellence. Bellcrest sell to a wide range of customers *whereas/while* Electrovans is still very dependent on one company for their trade.

Needham: Well, Sir Frederick, *although/while* I agree wholeheartedly with what you say, I think you have perhaps overlooked one or two points. Williams has the full backing of his staff *whereas/while* Downes has lost the support of some of his technical staff. Men like Orpenshaw don't like to see their projects abandoned even *while* they may appreciate the financial reasons for such measures. In fact, it is quite possible that Orpenshaw may transfer to Electrovans *although* this has not been settled yet. If he leaves Bellcrest, the company will find it difficult to develop this speed control *in spite of* having produced the original designs.

EPISODE 10

Exercise A

1 Downes told Malone that the findings of the preliminary survey did not *satisfy* him. As the findings did not *convince* him, he felt the study would not be enough to *persuade* the Board to back the SC1. He said he needed *hard facts* to *present* to the Board, not *rumours*. He added that the facts and figures in the survey were not *sufficient* on their own, and asked Malone to prepare a full report for *circulation* by 20th August.

2 Spence brought the *agenda* for the next Board meeting into Downes. As Downes didn't want to discuss the SC1, the *wording* of *item* four had to be *revised.* Downes did this so that Needham would have no chance of *raising* the *subject* of the SC1, and pressing for *details* of the project. He also told Spence to look up the *minutes* of the meeting at which the SC1 had been suspended in case he was unable to keep Needham off the *subject* of development projects.

3 When Needham raised the subject of the SC1 at the Board meeting, Downes confirmed that a major project was *under consideration.* He said he intended to *submit* his management's *recommendations* at the next Board meeting, when he hoped to be able to *table* a full *report* on the project. A more important *issue* to Downes was the source of the rumour Needham had heard.

4 Downes told Needham that the SC1 had been suspended five years before, not rejected, and Spence confirmed this by looking up the *relevant minute.* Mr March said, however, that Spence was *quoting* parts of a document *out* of *context* as the following sentence recommended that the patents and designs should be sold.

Exercise B

When Downes realized that Bellcrest's loan *was being reconsidered* by the Bank, he called a meeting of the management committee to discuss plans for diversification. The SC1 *was chosen* as the most promising new product. This device *had been invented* by Bob Orpenshaw several years before but the project *had been suspended* because of financial difficulties. There had been quite a controversy over the matter and Donald Williams, the Marketing Manager, *had been obliged* to resign because of it. Downes did not want to reveal Bellcrest's renewed interest in the SC1, until a market survey *had been carried out* by a firm of management consultants.

At the moment, this study *is being conducted* by M.P. Consultants. A preliminary survey *has just been completed* from the answers to questionnaires which *were sent out* some weeks previously. Downes *has now seen* this survey. He found it disappointing and decided not to mention the SC1 to the Board of Directors, although he *is continually being pressed* by the Bank to give them details of his development plans. M.P. Consultants *have been asked* to investigate rumours that Cremorne Cars are interested in manufacturing an electric car, and at the moment further enquiries *are being made.*

Exercise C

1 It was resolved to abandon work on the BX10.
2 It was suggested that all development projects should be reviewed.
3 It was decided to postpone discussion on the SC1 until the next meeting.
4 It was assumed that a full report would be ready by August 20th.

5 The Chairman was requested to table a full report on the SC1.
6 The SC1 was considered to be too expensive.
7 An increase in the Directors' fees was approved.
8 The Directors were requested to be more punctual.
9 It was resolved to diversify the product range within the near future.
10 The next meeting was arranged for September 2nd.

Exercise D Bellcrest had revived the SC1 project with a view to *diversifying* their product range. Electrovans were also interested *in marketing* a speed control device similar to the SC1. Both companies were eager *to get* financial support from Ashburnham's Bank. Donald Williams, the Managing Director of Electrovans, had already drawn up proposals *for developing* his product and he took every opportunity *of presenting/to present* his case to Sir Frederick Ashburnham. Maurice Downes, on the other hand, insisted *on treating* Bellcrest's project as confidential. He maintained that there was no point *in discussing* the plans until detailed information was available. Sir Frederick was unwilling *to decide* which firm to support. His assistant, Edward Needham, thought there was a good case *for investing* in Electrovans and he persisted *in drawing* Sir Frederick's attention to the advantages *of supporting* Williams. However, Sir Frederick was not prepared to *commit* himself.

EPISODE 11

Exercise A

1 Sir Keith Frisby was impressed by the *report* on the SC1. From the report he *judged* that Bellcrest had made an important technical *breakthrough.* Needham interrupted, and Downes insisted that Malone should be allowed to *explain* his report and *defend* his recommendations. Another Board member said that the report *stressed* the importance of electric vehicles, although no such market *existed* as yet.

2 After the demonstration, Needham *submitted* to the Board that the SC1 was not a *worthwhile* project. He stated that the Bank would not *advance* the money to launch it, and that the best *advice* he could give was for Bellcrest to *sub-contract* to a firm that was better *suited* to making such products.

3 One of the Board members wished to put a *motion* to the *effect* that the company should continue development of the SC1. He also suggested that the Chairman should look for the necessary *capital.* The *motion* was duly *seconded* and *passed* by a large majority. Needham did not *support* the *motion,* although he was the only one to *oppose* it.

Exercise B Downes believed (that) the SC1 was finished.
Malone complained (that) he wasn't giving him the support he needed.
Downes enquired/asked why the SC1 was going to be such a big production job. Malone explained that Orpenshaw had changed the specifications.
Downes added that the report was taking a long time. Malone admitted (that) he hadn't finished it. Downes suggested (that) Malone's wife had been rather indiscreet. Malone denied that his wife gave away company secrets. Downes wondered if the consultants were any good. Malone assured him (that) they

were a very sound firm. Downes felt (that) rumours really weren't enough. Malone regretted (that) he couldn't get anything in writing. Downes asked/enquired why he had to make such a secret of the demonstration. Malone disclosed that Cremorne Cars had agreed to let them carry out tests with their car. Downes maintained that there might not be any car for all they knew. Malone insisted that Cremorne Cars were intending to develop a commuter car.

Exercise C

1 He asked if I had seen Needham recently.
2 He wondered if/whether there was any chance of reviving the SC1.
3 He asked what time the meeting was.
4 He didn't know why the Bank was withdrawing the loan.
5 Spence wanted to know how the SC1 works/worked.
6 Needham doubted whether/if the SC1 was suitable.
7 He asked if/whether the report would be ready soon.
8 He wanted to find out who took the minutes.
9 He couldn't remember if/whether we/they had decided to sell the SC1.
10 He wasn't sure whether/if the meeting began at two or half past two.

Exercise D

Malone's first problem was production. If he had wanted to, Driver *could have insisted* on the impossibility of producing the SC1, but Malone *was able to persuade* him that production capacity could be increased sufficiently. Due to postponement of the discussion until the next Board meeting, Malone *was able to spend* more time on the report, but in spite of his efforts he *was not able/unable to convince* Downes. The Managing Director *could have abandoned* the SC1 at this point, but Malone *was able to get* permission to arrange a demonstration for the Board. Bad news from M.P. Consultants *could also have endangered* the project but fortunately Dr Perkins *was able to produce* some encouraging figures. All this meant that Malone *was able to put forward* a good case for the SC1. The Board agreed to support the project, although they *could so easily have rejected* it.

EPISODE 12

Exercise A

1 At the Board meeting Downes won the *approval* of his Board to *go ahead* with the SC1, provided that he could *raise* the money to *launch it.* Ashburnham's Bank, the obvious *source* of this money, seemed to be *backing* Electrovans so Downes rang Sir Frederick to arrange a meeting to discuss the whole matter.

2 Sir Frederick was glad to have the information on the SC1, as he could then *assess* Bellcrest's *claim* to the Bank's money. Downes told Sir Frederick he could argue Bellcrest's *claim* in detail against any *rivals* the Bank could *put up.*

3 Sir Frederick told his secretary to *arrange* an *appointment* with Downes for the following week. His secretary wanted to know what time would *suit* Downes, who told her that three o'clock on Wednesday would be *convenient.*

Exercise B

Urwin: Maurice, I almost got run down in the yard just now. I was walking over to the main office when this damn little car nearly took the pants off me. If he *had blown* his horn, I *would have heard* him and gotten out of the way.

Downes: My apologies. Sam, But if you *had looked/had been looking* where you were going, you *would have seen* him I expect.

Urwin: Well, if your drivers *race* around like that every day as they seem to be doing, you*'ll soon have* some accidents. Maybe if you *told* them to be careful, do you think they *would drive* a little slower?

Downes: Yes, if we *tell* our drivers to drive slowly then they*'ll do* it.

Urwin: If you *could* do that, I *would* be grateful.

Downes: We don't have accidents here, you know.

Urwin: If you *did have* an accident, it *would really wake you up*, wouldn't it.

Downes: O.K. I*'ll ask* Driver to see to it if you *think* its necessary.

Urwin: Thanks. Then if I *go out* again, maybe I *won't get* run over. And if you *had done* that before, I *wouldn't have been* in danger in the first place.

Exercise C

1 Present a strong case *so as to* be able to convince the Board.
2 Get hold of car *so* have to negotiate with Cremorne Cars.
3 Orpenshaw arrange demonstrations *so (that)* Board will see the advantages.
4 Brief Beeston *so* Jean will have to make an appointment for next week.
5 Must see Urwin *so* must find out which hotel he's in.
6 Forgot to give Driver report *so* figures have not been checked.
7 Write to Mandle *so as to* answer his questions.
8 Jean off sick *so* Betty must type letters.
9 Take car into garage *so (that)* engine can be repaired.
10 Downes says Jane indiscreet *so* must ask her about Needham.

Exercise D

1 Send six hundred of Item Number 527.
2 Meet the representative arriving on Pan American Flight 431 on Wednesday.
3 The President of Passlee Corporation says the deal is off. Arrange a meeting.
4 We need surge diverters urgently. Order 500.
5 The order we placed on the 8th of this month has not yet arrived. It is urgent that you attend to the matter.

EPISODE 13

Exercise A

1 Downes was unwilling to co-operate with Williams mainly because he had no *trust* in him. He was unable to *trust* a man who had clearly been less than *honest* in his dealings with Passlee Electronics. The events of five years previously had already destroyed any *goodwill* that might have existed between the two men and left an atmosphere of *mistrust*. Downes *had* no *confidence* in the *honesty* of Williams, so when he announced that Electrovans' speed control did not infringe Bellcrest patents, Downes certainly did not *take* this on *trust* and began to make enquiries about the matter.

His lack of confidence in their honesty was in the end well *justified* and Downes was glad he *put* his *trust* in his own judgement.

2 Downes was anxious that Electrovans should be merged with Bellcrest rather than becoming a *competitor* in the same field. Sir Frederick Ashburnham, however, was against a *merger* and preferred Electrovans to manufacture the speed control units as *sub-contractors* to Bellcrest. Downes opposed any such arrangement and continued to put the case for a *take-over*. He finally agreed to Sir Frederick's proposals on condition that Bellcrest should be *represented* on the Board of Electrovans by a completely *trustworthy* person.

Exercise B

1 Joy Banks can write a good story about Downes and Williams.
2 Malone may recognize Electrovans.
3 He can realize all his plans.
4 The Malones may move house.
5 Orpenshaw can concentrate on his technical work.
6 Now the Malones can buy a new car.
7 A new marketing manager may be appointed immediately.
8 Downes can speak to Electrovans' Managing Director now.
9 Beamish Motors may buy from Electrovans again.
10 The R. & D. section may be rehoused.

Exercise C

Downes: If you buy from Electrovans, Sam, our agreement with Passlee may *be terminated*.

Urwin: Now, don't blame me for going to Electrovans. It's your own fault, Maurice. I should *have been told* about the SC1 long ago.

Downes: But surely you see that it is necessary to keep it a secret? If our competitors had found out, it would *have been* bad for business.

Urwin: Keeping quiet about it has been even worse for business. This deal with Electrovans might never *have been considered* if you had trusted me with your secret. As it is I cannot *be expected* to reverse my decision now.

Malone: But, Sam, the SC1 is so much better than anything that could *be designed* by Electrovans.

Urwin: The Electrovans' design may not *be* better than the SC1, but at least they have the resources to put it on the market. You can't deny, Paul, that the SC1 cannot *be produced* without difficulty. And I just do not believe that their design infringes your patents. That must *have been checked* before they went ahead.

Malone: You don't know Williams. Anyway, Electrovans has just lost its biggest customer. Their ability to produce could *be affected* by this.

Urwin: If I had had this information earlier, I might *have been prepared* to cancel negotiations. But it is too late now. The contract should *be signed* the day after tomorrow.

Exercise D

1. Urwin was negotiating a deal with Electrovans *despite the fact that* he still had an agreement with Bellcrest.
2. Williams knew about the SC1 *whereas* Urwin hadn't been told.
3. Urwin wanted to buy the Electrovans' speed control *despite the fact that* Bellcrest could produce a better one.
4. Downes was pessimistic about Bellcrest's chances *whereas* Malone was rather more hopeful.
5. Electrovans was going ahead with its speed control *despite the fact that* it probably infringed Bellcrest patents.
6. Bellcrest intended to produce the SC1 *despite the fact that* it was right outside their normal field.
7. Electrovans were ready to produce a speed control *whereas* Bellcrest had only just decided to revive their project.
8. Bellcrest was in a strong position *whereas* Electrovans had just lost its biggest customer.
9. Downes is a sound man *whereas* Williams is very adventurous.
10. Downes agreed to launch the new project *despite the fact that* he is usually very cautious.